Variations
on a
Planet

Peter Brock

Pottersfield Press,
Lawrencetown Beach, Nova Scotia
1993

Canadian Cataloguing in Publication Data

Brock, Peter W.

> Variations on a planet
> ISBN 0-919001-77-7

> 1. Man — Influence on nature — Moral and ethical aspects. 2. Human ecology — Philosophy. 3. Brock, Peter W. I. Title

GF80.B76 1993   179.1   C93-098527-3

Cover painting by Peter Brock

Published with the financial support of the Nova Scotia Department of Tourism and Culture, the Canada Council and the Department of Communications.

Pottersfield Press
Lawrencetown Beach
R.R. 2, Porters Lake
Nova Scotia B0J 2S0

Tom Berry — mentor from afar
and
Laura — my daughter and friend

"Once we stop denying the crisis of our time and let ourselves experience the depth of our own responses to the pain of our world, the grief, or anger, or fear we experience cannot be reduced to concerns about our own skins."
Joanna Macy

VARIATIONS

First Words 7

Letter to Tom Berry 9

A Journey 11

Teachers 20

Brock's Law 25

Brock's Law Revisited 35

Getting Home 45

Good — but not Good Enough 51

A Silent Swerving 59

Lines to See By 66

Awakening from Nightmares 83

A Visit 88

The Fluid Oneness of Things 95

Balancing Act 103

The Chairman and the Chokerman 107

Dancing 114

Joe Said 120

Letter to my Daughter 122

Last Word 125

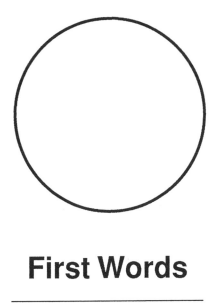

First Words

These words and sketches are an attempt to bring together some experiences with the planet, some thoughts about them, and a deeper sense of their music. The chapters are variations on a theme of the planet, and the book a sonata, if you like, for three 'voices'— body, mind, and spirit. The effort to combine the intimacy of personal experience with an intellectual search and the awe I feel for life have stretched me considerably. In fact, I was going to call the book "Stretching Exercises," but that sounded too much like a Jane Fonda book, rather than my own. The presence of slang and informal language, quotations and paraphrases, anger and empathy, may give pause but it is a full range of experience, ideas and feelings I am trying to convey. The sketches add another personal touch and are another way of being there — another variation.

Writing began in the sun near Georgian Bay in 1990, and several of the sketches are also from that land of pine, rock and big sky. It was completed in the brilliant colours of the fall of 1991 in Nova Scotia, as was the cover painting, "Huckleberry Hills." And it was fussed over and added to a bit after that. Some of it is enjoyable and some of it isn't.

Certain ideas, certain phrases even, are repeated, not so that you will remember them (an old teachers' ruse), but because they seem to run through everything. And that indeed illustrates one of them: that the universe is simple but endlessly complex. That is also why the book is called *Variations on a Planet*.

While Darwin comes in for a lot of flack, it is not personal. It is Darwinism that is found to be impoverished, whose roots are merely a reflection of Victorian thought. He just got the glory, which is what he wanted ("To he who convinces goes the glory" or words to that effect), and now the blame.

The book is about as thick as a book of poetry and perhaps that is a way it can be read. It is, like poetry, a web of experiences, ideas, and images. Some of it is relentless and intense, maybe even grumpy, but I hope that passion and humour squeeze through.

It is dedicated to my daughter along with all who struggle and delight in their own journey and to Tom Berry whose influence I have felt throughout. And it is a plea, joined to his, to "befriend the Earth."

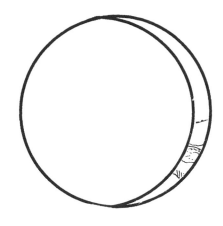

Letter to Tom Berry

Spring, 1992

Dear Tom,

At sea, not too long ago, we were running down buoys in the fog by dead reckoning. Been doing quite well really but the wind was rising and we missed the critical one. We hauled off the sails and motored back on the reciprocal heading for a while but still couldn't find it. There was a radio navigation beacon where we wanted to go so I got out the RDF [radio direction finder] and tuned it in. And we followed the null through the fog. The sounder showed we were approaching land and things were getting somewhat tense. Suddenly, we broke through into the sun and there ahead was the beacon. Our course was clear.

That story can serve as metaphor: being lost, the fog, the null (the peace!), the approaching danger, and you, perhaps, the beacon. But the truth is that when I heard you say, some years ago, we needed a "new story," the sun shone on a clearer course. Naturally, everything we do depends upon the story we know. It is all a matter of story.

The first really blinding flash I remember was Thomas Kuhn's book The Structure of Scientific Revolutions. *Fresh from a science degree, it stopped me cold. Kuhn said, in effect, science is a matter of story. It is one kind of story. History is another, politics, economics, yet more. And music, and art. And you, a Jesuit, told me that science tells a story we have never known before, that it is a sacred cosmic story of many* dimensions, that the story itself says the story is always changing and cannot go back, and that stories describe but cannot explain because the mystery remains. So that is why you use the word "story." Ah hah, as they say in Sweden. What a journey we're on, what an adventure, and what a story! An infinitely transforming mystery story with the cosmos as storyteller. Who but those asleep, or dead, would want it any other way?

I have, I know now, been trying to tune in to the story all my life but the static and clutter has made reception difficult. A limp excuse perhaps — man is not a rational but a rationalizing animal who later makes excuses — but it is clearer now. Thanks for being there then. You didn't even know.

May I quote some of your own words? "We need to know the story in all its resonances, in all its meanings. The universe story is the divine story, the human story, the story of the trees, the story of the rivers, of the stars, the flowers, the planets, everything. There is nothing else. It is as simple as a kindergarten tale, yet as complex as all cosmology and all knowledge and all history." Now why didn't I hear that when I was ten? Then again maybe I did, though faintly.

Teachers appear when the student is ready! A couple of shepherds (and dogs), the odd fisherman, woodsman, Native North Americans, and a few artists have given me the feeling they belonged to the planet. Never before have I felt the clear weight of your intellectual and spiritual dimension. But what struck me most of all on meeting you for the first time was that there was no hint of a hidden agenda, only a profound sense that the message came through you not from you.

Thanks for the beacon. It started me writing these words and as the fog cleared from my path I saw it more clearly. Your guidance is reflected in all that follows.

With thanks,

Peter

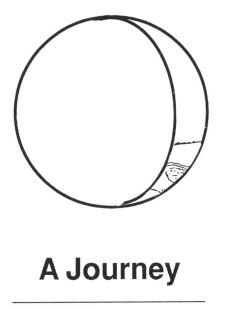

A Journey

Thirteen days on the North Atlantic under sail brings you back to basics, as I recently discovered during a crossing from Bermuda to the Azores on a 40-foot steel ketch. The trip had all the features I had imagined from an early age: bright sun and driving rain, starlit nights, and nights of an almost active blackness when the boat sprouted wings of phosphorescence, fine food, some of which I lost, and wind. All kinds of wind, most of it strong. It was a fast, tough, enjoyable sail on an able boat and we kept her moving.

There was plenty of time to reflect and to just be — not to read, not to intellectualize, not to write, not to fuss, but just to be. The twelve to three watch one night was clear and brilliant with the Milky Way above and stars to the horizon. Each glance at the windex on the top of the main mast took one out to the vastness of space. A physicist in the late 1800s, before Einstein, before Heisenberg, wrote that it appeared that the universe was infinite in all directions. Look out and look in, you'll see what he meant. He was condemned, of course, but we are coming back to those once heretical ideas. Gazing upwards at the night sky I was reminded of the Jesuit priest, Pierre Teilhard de Chardin, who lay one similar night in 1914 in the trenches of war-torn France gazing at the sky. Amidst the horror of the First World War he was perhaps the first to envision an emerging transformation of human consciousness and the first perhaps as a scientist and a priest to envision the integration of the two into a new perception of being. The existentialist fashion of my youth, the philosophy of Camus and Sartre, which I always mistrusted, is easy to fall into while gazing at the night sky. We seem so insignificant, so overwhelmed by the "infinity" of space. Teilhard turned it around and brought it, not back to our physical selves, not back to our egocentric view of ourselves, but back to our conscious-ness. He knew as a scientist that the evolutionary path was towards increasing complexity with one level based upon, and transcending, the one before. He reasoned that evolution from the simplicity of space to increasing complexity on earth brought a new focus on our own consciousness, that indeed, evolution created life and consciousness (or the other way round!) and that we are the expression of that increasing complexity, the eyes, ears and awareness of the universe. Fifteen billion years have brought us through the most extraordinary and the most sacred transfor-mations to self-reflective consciousness — totally awesome, as the kids used to say.

We are the first generation in fifteen billion years to have the empirical evidence that the earth's story is more complex than even the most mystical of holy men dreamed. From energy, to matter, to life, to consciousness, from the exquisite timing of the "big bang", the invention of photosynthesis, and the creation of flowers, the transformations of evolution have brought forth life and life's awareness of life.

Father Thomas Berry, who calls himself a 'geologian', is the inheritor of Teilhard's mantle and it was perhaps because I had talked to him just before I left that these thoughts came to me that starlit night. Towards the end of the watch there was a bright light that I thought was a ship approaching from the east. I watched intently so I could inform the next watch of its position and course but it rose slowly until, when it was ten degrees above the horizon, I realized it was Venus.

I have been involved in education for thirty years and there is a lot of talk these days about the need for reform. There are no accidents, and education, like society, is but a reflection of ourselves. We perceive the world based upon "sets" derived from our experience but behind the sets, underlying how we think the world works and how we construct our experience is an even more basic model: the way in which we see ourselves and the relationship between ourselves and everything else. This fundamental model conditions *all* thought, *all* perception, and *all* action. The most common self model is that of an individual self quite separate from the rest of the world, a skin encapsulated ego. What is inside the skin is *me* and what is outside is *not me*. This view, challenged by Buddha and indeed Christ, was challenged again by Teilhard because he was able to bring some of the insights and discoveries of science to bear. His vision has been confirmed in the intervening seventy years by an emerging earth story upon which we can build a new ground, a new basis for our perceptions to transform our view of ourselves. Education, like everything we do and think, is based upon our view of ourselves. In this sense, reform with our old sets intact, like changing watches on a sinking boat, is insufficient. It does not need to be reformed but transformed, as do we.

Sailing has always been a way for me to leave the intellect behind and just be. Hiking out on my Laser, immersed in being at one with the wind and waves, in being of the earth not just on the earth allows me to glimpse another self beyond the skin encapsulated ego. T.S. Eliot speaks of it as "music heard so deeply that it isn't heard at all, but you are the music while it lasts." The immense sky and the intuitions of Teilhard reaffirmed that sense as Venus rose to precede the day.

The next night I had three to six, my favourite watch. It brought the new day and heading east, I needed sun glasses at five o'clock. It was easy to understand the ancient pre-Copernican view of the sun going around the earth, to see the sun "rising." But as the anomalies grew it was inevitable, fight it though we did, that the shift was made and the sun became the centre of our universe, and that view became part of a new consciousness. It was not reality that changed so painfully but, with more information, it was our perceptions which changed. The new perceptions didn't change the world but they did change how we thought and acted.

We are in the midst of a new Copernican revolution, a shift from the individual ego as the centre of our inner universe to the true self as the "still point of a turning world," to quote Eliot again. We must add to our awareness of individuality an equally real awareness of unity with the whole. Oneness and separateness become but different expressions of the same thing. This change of consciousness has become an evolutionary imperative.

After a few days out, the dolphins came. One day they just arrived to play "chicken" with the bow. Suddenly they were there and others came racing from all directions to investigate the fun, converging on us at twenty knots leaping six feet clear in a kind of joyous whoop. They almost winked at us and one show-off jumped and turned sideways again and again landing with a great splash. You could feel his grin. They certainly have fun. In *The Happiness Purpose*, DeBono proposes that humour is more important than reason in his book: "Humour arises directly from that process of perception that allows the mind to switch over and look at something in a completely new way." Humour, of the kind he is talking about, is produced by a surprise change of context. *How do you spell ptarmigan?* With a silent p as in swimming. In most cases, at the level of ego defence and the maintenance of our perceptions, a change of context is threatening and we react fearfully. But that is exactly what we must do ... change the context in which we see ourselves. Among the many paradoxes of life, one dolphin seems to personify "loosen up, this is serious."

Indeed, paradoxes are the spice of life which befuddle us and keep us guessing and on edge. And they are hard for a western mind to reconcile since we are used to either/or concepts. F. Scott Fitzgerald suggested a sign of intelligence is the ability to hold two opposing points of view and still function. How can something be serious but demand humour? How can something be separate but united? There are no boundaries other than those we create ourselves — it is context alone that is important. And the context is always changing, as is life.

How is it possible to feel so connected to the planet when alone at sea, to know the sense of oneness and at the same time to be so separate? A difficult concept but one with a fifteen-billion-year history. The idea of evolution being the path to increasing complexity with levels which depend upon but transcend the ones before is as obvious as the sun but we seem almost to deny the evidence. Molecules need atoms, cells need molecules, organisms need cells ... it's simple. In the same sense, the ego derived from our separate experiences of life is but an aspect of a larger self at one with the world. We are indeed separate but that is not all we are.

I must admit, with the skipper standing at the main mast reefing in the rising wind, knee deep in solid water, it was difficult to tell the difference between him and all that surrounded him. There was a full force ten storm off Newfoundland that was affecting all of the North Atlantic and we were getting it in the face ... and boots. We had a GPS (Global Positioning System) on board and it was fascinating, miraculous even, to use three satellites to find our position within a boat's length, to measure time to the nanosecond while crashing about on the ocean. The very symbol of modern technology, the computer, provides a curious example of the no-boundary condition so essential to our new perceptions. The whole thing depends upon on/off circuitry but what is on if there is no off? Or what is up if there is no down? Or, God knows, what is the crest of a wave if there is no trough twenty feet below? They are but aspects of the same thing. We make them separate but they are not. We make ourselves separate but we are not. What is this planet but permutations of positive and negative charges and what is one without the other? Reason tells us on is not off, that they are separate, but the process that is exemplified by humour, of swiftly shifting contexts, tells us they are but aspects of the same thing. Bring on the dolphins.

Where do they go when it really blows? And where do we go? That night watch was something else, and the next night for that matter. It was dark, dark, with thirty-five-knot winds. We were comfortable, secure in ourselves, but excited. Alone in the night, black sea and white sparkling waves of phosphorescence, the wind shrieking above the roar of our passage. It was pure adventure, pure exhilaration. We could have been worried, I guess, complaining about the wet or the violent motion. What's the fun in that? And besides, the sea conditions would not have changed any more than the world did after Copernicus. It seems to me that a sense of adventure is what we need to cope with the changing world and the metaphor of a voyage is appropriate. But it must be your own voyage, not a guided bus tour. Almost everyone recognizes that the world is in crisis but there is a common reluctance to recognize and celebrate the full involvement of the human race in its own evolution.

The threshold is not out there ahead of us somewhere, a line from which we might conceivably draw back. We are well across it. To say we are not ready is like saying a teenager is not ready for puberty. It did not happen overnight but the evidence now crowds around us; we are obliged to know what we do in the world, to see that it has changed and that we are participants in the change. One of the great curiosities of human civilization is that we have moved so far into this age without acknowledging we were doing so. We are truly out of the garden but there are only dim reflections of the larger problem, which is that we literally do not know what we are doing.

True, there is danger, and we have added handsomely to the stock of danger in the world, but there is also opportunity. We are in new terrain and a first step in any direction is to acknowledge and accept that. It is a time of great choice and possibility, yet fraught with danger; a time of adventure in every sense of the word, and the greatest one that any of us will ever see. If the contemplation of the tasks before us is not to be utterly crushing to the human spirit we need to see them in a light that makes them bearable. Adventure, while recognizing danger, carries with it the banner of hope. Forty-eight hours later we put on more sail and the dolphins returned. Shearwaters and petrels, dainty as flakes of soot, had been with us throughout, or we with them, or all of us together.

Bermuda was a long way astern. It remained in my memory as an island which seemed curiously purposeless. Under each grove of trees there was junk in the undergrowth, the detritus of consumer society. Men and black-backed gulls hung around the refuse tips. The green was golf courses. My image was one of spectator living, the planet as entertainment. The Azores appeared like faint clouds straight ahead. How could we miss with GPS? Terraced fields rose up the steep hills, habitations strung like necklaces around the contours. I lived ashore for a few days, walking the island from one end to the other. It was alive with people tilling soil, milking cows, riding donkeys, fishing, talking in the sun. Although it was like being in the nineteenth century, I met a man who had a Macintosh computer in his office and a fisherman with a GPS.

The island was alive with flowers too. I have never seen such colour, such profusion. There was a time without flowers. Can you imagine? It is an image Tom Berry talks of. The time of the creation of flowers, one of the sacred transformations of earth's evolutionary path. It was vivid there on the Azores.

There was something else that struck me forcibly — a sense of being of the earth not just on it. This was not romantic back-to-nature nostalgia — it was not a question of donkeys or the nineteenth century — it was real, active, dynamic, and of the present. And perhaps, in the sense of consciousness, of the future.

There is evidence, growing daily, that people are beginning to glimpse their essential oneness in an intellectual way but that is a long way from its becoming the core, the deepest sense of ourselves, of our existence. How do we make that journey forward? How do we move from spectator on an island of existence to being of the earth — from Bermuda to the Azores? Humour, knowledge, adventure, awareness, openness, and practice, practice, practice. It's not easy and it's not far out; it is as close as we are to ourselves and as necessary as breathing.

And how do we use these insights to transform education and ourselves? "When all else fails, read the instructions" as they say, and the instructions are there for us to read in the earth story if we become earth literate. Begin with the pattern of evolution, a dynamic process in which one level is based upon but transcends the one below. That is a very important fact — not theory, fact.

Schooling began, quite recently really, as a way of transmitting information — it is knowledge-based. Knowledge tends to become static, to become an end in itself, takes on aspects of the absolute and becomes the preserve of experts. Evolution, levels depending upon but transcending those below, gives guidance here. Knowledge is good; it was necessary, is necessary, but is no longer good enough. It is not that knowledge is not needed but in a dynamic world, process takes precedence over "facts" because "facts" change now as they did in Copernicus' time, or the time of flowers. Teachers do not need to know it all, indeed cannot, but can be guides and fellow travellers. Whew. What a relief! It is a pretty precarious existence being a know-it-all. There can be no more teachers in the old sense, people who pour in knowledge — that isn't working — but only people who provide opportunities for learning. That's a change and it is very difficult to get used to. Having come to know but also being in the process of knowing … now there's the beef. That's a role for a "teacher," not as a font of knowledge but as a guide to the process of knowing. It is a radical and profound change where risk is necessary, mistakes important, and questions more important than answers. Think about it. The inevitable process of evolution and surely an adventure of the finest kind.

And what do we need to know about? Ourselves, the universe, and our place in it. As Tom Berry describes it, "It's all a question of story. We are in trouble now because we are between stories. The Old Story — the account of how the world came to be and how we fit into it — sustained us for a long time. It shaped our attitudes, provided us with life purpose, energized action, consecrated suffering, integrated knowledge, and guided education. We awoke in the morning and knew where we were. We could answer the questions of our children. But now it is no longer functioning and we have not yet learned the New Story."

That 'new' story, as old as time, is the ground of our being and is there to be read, and give guidance, in the earth and in the fifteen-billion-year cosmic story.

Now this is all very well, very fancy, but where do we start? It seems to me there are two guiding principles to transform ourselves and education. The first is to celebrate and acknowledge our uniqueness and diversity. The 'instructions' of the last billion years show that symbiosis — autonomy and mutual support — is a guiding principle of all life. To honour in your own life this *fact* of life means simply to foster self-respect and self-esteem, in yourself and others, and to offer this honour and esteem to all life. As a teacher, this is by far the greatest offering one can make to students — by far. And it's not such a bad idea for friends and lovers either.

To grow beyond the skin encapsulated ego which demands such enormous support from the planet caused by our sense of separateness leads to the second guiding principle — to celebrate and acknowledge our oneness and communion by fostering the idea of service, not to our individual selves but to the planet. The world does not owe us a living, but we owe the world a living. This is an idea as difficult for us as was once the idea that the sun was the centre of our galaxy. It is here that practice comes in, for it is in the practice of acting connected that one becomes so, in the act of serving that one is served. Here is the real revolution, surpassing the Russian, the French, the American, even the Copernican. It is more in the nature of the coming of the flowers. It is profoundly simple and terrifyingly complex.

It is said that people go mad in a herd and come to their senses one by one. I guess that is where we have to start. The winds of change are blowing. It's your watch.

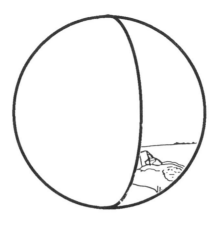

Teachers

I was not the kind of boy who took legs off insects and watched them struggle in agony. I was more interested in just watching them. I guess we all have to try the power trip at some time but I learned an early lesson about that from my dog. We were down in the ravine near the house and came across a baby crow which had fallen from the nest. It couldn't fly. I tried to 'sic' the dog on it, to kill it, I presume. He picked it up and shook it and put it down and looked at me. He hadn't done the job. I encouraged him again and he did it again. I recall now how gently he did it, but at the time I was annoyed he wouldn't get fierce the way dogs are supposed to. I shouted at him, I forced him on and on but it finally came through to me that he wouldn't and I shouldn't. I do not know what turned it around for me but somehow I saw it differently. We all stopped and just sat there under the tree in the growing dusk — the baby crow, which was virtually unharmed, my dog, and I. It was dark when I got home. I have no idea what I thought then, if I thought at all, but I have had a kinship with all life ever since. It was a lesson well taught and well learned. I was ten.

Only now do I understand a far deeper meaning of the experience, one I learned then without knowing it and which has governed my life ever since. Learning depends upon your own mindfulness and awareness; lessons are all around and all you have to do is to be open to them.

I have learned a lot from dogs over the years but perhaps my greatest teacher was my old Border collie, Sweep. He wasn't my dog really. He belonged to Henry, the owner of the sheep farm I was working on in Scotland. I was completely new to the game — had no idea really. I was told I could use Sweep if he would work for me. It was a good gamble and no one imagined he would, especially the owner. Sweep was thirteen, had been partially crippled by a Land Rover, and was set in his ways. Nevertheless, he was obliging and anxious to please as are all Border collies.

The farm was 15,000 acres of rough hill with 3,000 ewes and their lambs scattered and invisible to an untrained eye. When we needed to work with them, they had to be gathered in. This was not casual exercise. We began on the heights naturally, and each of us took a part of the hillside to be gathered, trying to converge with our sheep at the fank (pen) in the valley. We expected to gather about 500 each time and so work through the flock. Sweep was happy to come with me, after we put a rope on him, when we all set out separately to gather the sheep. I had been working and gathering for a while with Duncan, the owner's son, and knew what the orders were and how to go about it. Sweep and I, at last alone and he freed from his rope, got to the point where we were to begin our gathering.

I saw a sheep way off to the right and did the appropriate thing: stood parallel to the direction Sweep was to go, put my arm and staff out and said "Get away b'y." He smiled at me. *You're a nice guy but if you think I'm going over there, you're crazy.* I shouted, I beat my stick on the ground. He still smiled at me. In the nicest way he told me to take my orders and stuff them. *If you want to get away b'y, go ahead.* What is a man to do? I put Sweep on the rope again and began to run. That day I gathered the sheep.

It became hot work and I left my jacket on the hill by the burn. After the gathering and the dosing we turned the sheep back to their hill. I was too exhausted to care about my jacket but Duncan wandered off to get it, saying I'd need it for the next hill tomorrow and we wouldn't be back there for a month. He also said he didn't think I was very fit. I was too proud to admit I had run over fifteen miles on rough hill but I think he knew.

The same thing happened the next day, and the next. By then Sweep was unroped and came with me as I did "his" work. I remember his smile changed: *You're getting the hang of it now.*

After a week he began to hunt a little when we had a few sheep together. This is what dogs do, "hunting" back and forth behind the sheep to keep the group together once they have been gathered. He kept smiling. I was getting fitter.

At the end of the second week he "went b'y" a few sheep on his own which I hadn't seen. *Keep your eyes open, these sheep are smart and will get behind you if you don't watch it.* And I'm sure now I heard him say, *They only get stupid when they are fenced in — like people.* We began to get something going together — a partnership. It gave me the greatest pleasure. Few words were spoken. I had often only to point with my staff and Sweep was gone. When he saw I was prepared to work and to learn from him, he taught me the hill and how to work sheep. And his smile changed again. He no longer smiled at me. We smiled together. It was one of the greatest lessons I ever learned.

After a month we tried an experiment. Back at the first gathering place, five shepherds with their dogs, everyone with three but me, we set out alone to our posts. Not a word was spoken to any dog. We all went our separate ways. Sweep, unbidden, came with me. He had won the bet for me.

I got a young female pup called Gay. She was a moody enthusiast taken to running home if she screwed up. Sweep took over there, too, and with patience and energy taught Gay that she was good and that he would fix things if she messed up — for a while. Sweep gentled her into a good worker.

Then I got a "hunting" dog called Roy. He wouldn't go around sheep, could only hunt back and forth behind them and drive them forward — a kind of manager if you like. He was stupid and aggressive. Neither Sweep nor Gay liked him much but were happy to let him think he was doing the important work while they were off doing the creative stuff. It worked out OK. Sweep had nothing to teach Roy because Roy couldn't even understand anything but managing, which Sweep found easy and boring. But one day he did show Roy and me a thing or two. We were moving a few sheep from a barnyard, with a high stone fence around it, down the road to a new field of rape. We gathered them up and moved out with Roy all purposeful and in control. The sheep went out the gate and turned right — the wrong way. They took off with the taste of succulent greens in mind. Roy didn't know what to do but Sweep got around them and turned them back. I hadn't closed the gate so, of course, on their way back they went into the yard again.

Try again. We got organized and began to move towards the gate. Where is Sweep? Where is that dog now that I need him? The sheep were pressing towards the gate. Where was he? Then they began to run for the opening. Where was that damn dog? I screamed at him to come. No sign of him. Roy was pushing them on. They rushed out the gate — and turned left, the correct way. How did that happen? When we got them all through the gate, I found Sweep sitting on the road to the right, again with that rueful smile. *Sorry I couldn't come.* Sheep are creatures of habit and would have turned the same way again but he had cleared a six-foot stone dyke and got them going the right way. He sure got through to me, but I don't think Roy had a clue, or even noticed. Straight ahead — any way will do.

On Saturdays we gathered the rough woodland by the sea. It was sport. The sheep were wild and canny. We would catch them in place and dose them or inoculate them, see to their feet or whatever. It needed great dogs. I left Roy behind. The sheep knew the woods better by far than we did, but not better than Sweep did. One day he and Gay were with me and we found three ewes with two lambs. They took off and Sweep took off. I found him fifteen minutes later with the sheep on a rock outcrop with nowhere to go but down or back through the dog. This time I swear he was laughing. Later Henry and I happened to be going after the same ewe and she decided to swim to Ireland. "She's a gonner, leave her be," Henry said. But without thinking I called

Sweep and said "Get away b'y there you old bugger." He took to the ocean and turned the ewe. Henry and I stared with our mouths open. It became part of the folk lore of the farm. No one had ever seen a dog swim around a ewe. I didn't know any better and Sweep was teaching again. New things are possible — just try. Henry said Sweep was truly my dog now. But Sweep and I knew it was the other way round.

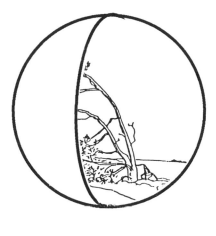

Brock's Law

If Murphy, whoever he was, can have a law, and Peter can have a principle, then I, whoever I am, can have a law. Brock's Law states, "The answer is never where you find the question." You cannot solve a problem at the level you find it. Or, you always find the answer in a different place from the problem. There are many ways to put it. If Brock's Law is understood it will explain Murphy's Law except in cases of outright stupidity which are explained by the Peter Principle. In fact they are both explained by the law and failure to understand the law, brings them both into play!

Brock's law appears to be a universal law. Problem solving at its own level is impossible and attempts to do so only delay resolution and understanding. This seems to be hard to grasp in our culture. In fact, when first I thought of it, it seemed somewhat silly and a bit cynical. But the law applies from the spiritual to the mundane, the sacred to the profane.

A couple of wildly separate examples, one sublime and one trivial, will show (prove) the law and demonstrate the way in which a solution attempted at the level of the problem comes, in the end, from outside its definition.

Niels Bohr, whose son had stolen a pipe from a local shop, was musing on the impossibility of considering his son in the light of love and justice. His brooding set him thinking about the vase and the faces in the well known figure-ground drawing in which you can see only one at a time, either the face or the vase, though they are both the same drawing. This led him to consider the physics problem he was absorbed in attempting to describe light as a wave or a particle, both of which seemed to be possible. And his musing later became the idea of complementarity in quantum physics, that opposites are complementary descriptions of the same reality. It was a revolution whose answer did not come from the narrow focus of physics where the problem had been defined. It could not have. Later he was to say, "How wonderful that we have met with paradox. Now we have some hope of making progress." Bohr understood the law. Enigma fosters discovery.

John Sculley, who is now CEO of Apple Computers, was once with Pepsi and tried to take on Coke. He tried everything he could to beat them at their own game but could not make a dent. Coke controlled the market because of its unique bottle and all other soft drinks were packaged in the same size bottles — an unexamined convention. Sculley then changed the rules of the game they were playing, as well as the size of the bottle, and began to win. It worked because he moved outside the context of the market defined and controlled by Coke. Enter the Pepsi generation. Now, they're neck and neck. From the profound to the trivial indeed! Or perhaps the sublime to the ridiculous — but the law seems to apply.

An appropriate and emotional example illustrates the law and how it can be used effectively. A feminist stance is a logical and understandable linear response to male chauvinism. But the two are simply two poles of the same quality. Attempting to solve the problem at the level you find it results only in stalemate. Transcending the problem to a human level, which of course includes male and female with no boundary, eliminates the stalemate and allows solutions. The same applies to problems of race.

This illustrates a profound feature of the law — that it can work for you or against you. Knowledge of it leads you on to new levels and solutions and lack of understanding of the law leaves you stuck — but convinced you have a solution — which leads only to deeper problems. Understanding the law transforms it into a useful law. Denying it makes it a dangerous and dead end law. You can tell which, dangerous or useful, by how elaborate the solutions are — and how expensive. It is impossible to imagine how complex and expensive this man/woman thing will get if separate battle stations are maintained, and how simple, even pleasant, the solutions are if they are abandoned.

The down side of the law always seems to hold in our culture, which surprises me although that is what good laws are supposed to do. But there are some required preconditions which ensure that the law applies and will catch you every time. They are as follows levels or categories exist but are not connected to one another and things can be described by their parts. These precepts are at the base of our culture and we know them to be true.

Just looking around at the way we try to solve problems illustrates the law. In the fisheries the problem is, obviously, not enough fish. The solution, at the level you find the problem (that is, numbers of fish) is to get better information about stock numbers and populations and set quotas on the number of fish caught. Then institute patrols to catch those who catch too many and make them throw them back — dead or alive. Simple. This is what we do. The answer is not there, as any fisherman knows. Brock's Law applies. Monitoring numbers only permits us to monitor extinction. Spruce Budworm a problem? That's easy — kill them. And after more than fifty years of spraying the budworm is still with us and the result — fewer spruce trees in proportion to fir, their main target. A sort of medicare for the poorer, weaker species resulting in a reduction of the more valuable one and in fact provision of *more* food for the budworm. Uh-oh.

The list to demonstrate the law is endless. Too much work? Work harder, get a phone in your car so you can work there too and not have time to think at all. Traffic congestion? Build more roads. New roads get congested? Build more. Want peace? Prepare for war. Crack users break the law? Create more laws and enforce them better. You're too fat? Go on a miracle diet but just keep on watching that ole TV. Technology causing problems? Why, more technology's the answer. Everywhere you look, whether in science or human affairs, you will find the conditions in which the law prevails and surprises. You hear people say, "It's always something." (Meaning something wrong.) It's the dreaded law.

The law has several categories, as all good laws should; first is the category of data, second is the category of poles or opposites, and a third is the category of symptoms or of a single pole. Where the problem is seen as data and the answer is sought with more data, then the law applies. Where the problem is seen as opposites and ways to "balance" the poles are sought the law also applies. Where the problem is a symptom and the attempt to solve it denies the cause or even that another pole exists then the law applies. In all three cases the law applies in a negative way.

In the matter of data, Brock's Law says that mere data does not bring insight, or solutions. Darwin is a good example and some people have observed that he might have gone on collecting data until his death had not Wallace provided him with the insight. (Which, in fact, his own grandfather could have done.) And Wallace did not have as much data as Darwin did! We have whole industries and institutions producing data for problems which do not need more data for solution. They are growth industries and very expensive ones. But then if your business is data, who wants answers?

In the matter of opposites, the tendency of describing something by its parts brings the law into effect. The way to soften the law and make it useful requires reconciling the opposites and recognizing that there are no boundaries other than the ones we make ourselves. A problem defined by opposites is solved by acknowledging that there is no boundary between the opposites and then moving to another level. Opposites are, in fact, but parts of the same reality, like Bohr's faces and complementarity in quantum theory.

There are two apparent paradoxes here that need to be explained. The matter of opposites is one, the matter of levels the other. That opposites are only parts of the same thing, as Bohr's faces indicated, is a hard one which depends upon a no-boundary concept quite foreign to our culture. This becomes somewhat weird and Bohr's complementarity seems more like eastern mysticism. But can you find a flaw? Bohr couldn't and no one has since. There isn't one. The concept of no boundary helps make the law useful in the case of opposites which allows them to be fused and transcended.

The matter of levels is another seeming paradox needing resolution for the law to be useful, not destructive. To describe the law requires the establishment of a hierarchy so that problems at one level can be solved at another level. This of course requires levels. One of the conditions for which the law holds in its dead-end or surprise mode is that levels are not connected, which our culture suggests is the case.

If, on the other hand, the levels are understood as levels of complexity which depend upon and are built upon those below then the law can lead to solutions and can be useful. Levels as separate categories harden and hide the law, but levels as degrees of complexity of the same thing soften and reveal it. This really makes the levels paradox the same as the paradox of opposites which is that there are no levels and no opposites and no boundaries though we also need and have both. Got it? It's very Buddhist.

Can you hold two opposing ideas at the same time and still function, which is F.Scott Fitzgerald's definition of intelligence? Well, to describe the law and to use it requires that you do. To describe the law requires levels and opposites. To use the law requires transcending the levels where problems are found and accepting that opposites are the same reality. Here the Peter Principle is revealed for what it is — the inability to be aware of, or sometimes even acknowledge, the existence of transcendent levels. You have reached "the level of your incompetence" as described by the Peter Principle when you cannot or do not want to see any more levels, or to look deeper.

There is a point here that needs to be emphasized in regard to using the law effectively which is made clearer by an understanding of evolution. Not Darwinian but post-Darwinian evolution. It is simple but complex and relates to both the data and the pole conditions. Evolution is dynamic (which Darwin did describe) and moves towards complexity. Each stage in the spectrum of complexity transcends but depends upon the stage below, or the less complex state.

This is self-evident and therefore difficult to see. Molecules need atoms, cells need molecules, organisms need cells etc. If you imagine that cells can be fully described by describing only their molecules, that the parts account for the whole, then the law will certainly apply. The point needs to be made, and made again, because data and molecules are absolutely necessary, as are poles and levels. Without cells there would be no organisms and without data and levels one could not go beyond them. The law simply states that answers are found beyond but do not dispense with the levels at which questions are defined.

The third category of symptoms is a troublesome but pervasive one and it should remain a separate category although it includes the other two categories. It is, for instance, where one finds the problems in the medical profession or agriculture, where symptoms are isolated and treatment attempted. It includes denying one pole and piling up all the data and effort at the other. As an example we know little of health but a lot about sickness. Wealth is all but frugality is invisible. And technology itself falls into this category since we seem quite unable to consider less technology! New technology is always introduced with a best case scenario and with profit as the motive. But the best case is *never* achieved and the worst case is left to the others to sort out — often with another best case scenario — thus making the problems worse! A Bill of Rights seems now to be a predominant focus throughout the world, but the solution consists of treating symptoms. It denies the opposite pole of responsibility and cannot help but trip over the law. In these cases, where an opposite pole is not in evidence, even stalemate is impossible and the cure is usually worse than the disease.

How did we get to the point where Brock's Law comes into play so forcefully and how can we make the law useful and not harmful?

We got there somewhat unwittingly and it took us a long time. One has to examine the further reaches of the law and move away from the mundane (as the law itself indicates). One place to look is science, since a lot of questions these days are thought to be scientific. Another place is learning, another economics, another law itself, yet another sex, and still another religion.

Science holds that a thing can be described by its parts. The aim of science is, in effect, to purge information of its context and discount personal experience as hearsay. Science and technology believe themselves to be neutral and proud of it. This approach settles like dust over all we do and think. But wait. Is science really mere data and the methods of science but to reduce things to their parts? That's the way it seems. Science discounts context and scientists discount … themselves. But meaning is found only in context and human experience. Obviously the law holds.

Can one find meaning in science while eliminating it? Can one gain insight by removing context? That sounds like the condition of opposites and it is. Get the facts and leave the context out of it, deny that context determines facts. Setting science and context apart fulfils the conditions that make the law destructive. Science has fallen into a deep trap. Unsatisfied with its legitimate role of description it proclaims that it can explain. Try to explain the unexplainable and the law will get you every time.

As it turns out, science is heavily value laden, as is technology, and the resolution to the dilemma is simply to acknowledge it. This leads to a new kind of science, as George Wald and Barbara McClintock know, and Bohr and Heisenberg knew. Nature can be revealed only in our relations with it and phenomena can be known only in their context.

Learning is connected to science by its methods and with the same results. We study math, chemistry, history, etc., etc. The difficult part of integration, of understanding process and meaning is left out, as though learning as well as science was neutral. But what could be more human than the search for a deeper understanding, what could be more human than learning? Learning is, like science, value-laden, both in what we learn and what we leave out. It is subjective, entirely within the knower, and the resolution is the same: integrate data and contexts — transcend mere data. Learning at the level of mere data, that is merely knowing *more*, is an unwinnable and futile struggle, and the law applies forcefully if that is all we do.

Economics abdicates all but limited solutions of any kind but at least admits to "externalities", thereby making it a sure bet to uphold the law's worst aspects. But economics is infected by a far more fundamental dishonesty — it doesn't know the meaning of its own terms, gross and net, capital and interest. The established order has *always* required subsidies: from peasant or slave, Aztec or Inca, Cherokee or Iroquois, from women, and always, always from the planet. But now it has come to pass that it is demanding subsidies from its own children while at the same time severely reducing their ability to pay. Economics, as presently conceived, reveals the most sinister face of Brock's Law where new solutions only create greater problems.

The legal system itself provides an obvious example in the category of opposites. It is purposely set up as adversarial, as a battle between opposites — justice brought to you by people who believe that means are separate from ends. It is no surprise Niels Bohr mused on love and justice. Imagine the consequences if the two were fused, not just mused upon, and justice became love.

Sex — ah yes. Male and female as complementary and not opposing poles eliminates the down side of the law. Gloria Steinem herself has come to see the human problem of self esteem buried deep in the trenches behind the battle stations. Sex is not a problem anyway. It is a delight but more importantly a solution. Without its invention we wouldn't be here. (The ever-present tension between man and woman perhaps deserves a personal note since my wife occasionally calls me a feminist, though probably not because I often iron her blouses. But I am not. I am merely bewildered by chauvinism, or fundamentalism of any kind, and concerned with the human presence within the earth community.)

Religion has traditionally been the place where mankind has tried to find a meaning for existence though it long ago rejected the sacredness of the planet. It has also long been disconnected from, even opposed to science. And although science too denies other ways of knowing and is unable to cope with the unprecedented, can one really just quarantine the two? Again we see a battle of conflicting opposites, of conflicting explanations . And can one leave nature out as though it was just background? Brock's Law, in the category of opposites, applies when man and nature are kept separate, when science and religion are kept separate, when nature and religion and man are kept separate.

Answers will not be found in man alone, in science alone, nor in religion alone. In the post-Darwinian concept of evolution progress is described neither by lonely selfishness (can one resist the quip that Darwin was frightened, lonely and selfish, hence his theory?) nor by the grand plan of an external intelligence. If we reject those extremes then we are left with something far more profound and far more magical and mysterious. That synergy, that interaction and interdependence, and that deliberate co-operation among different life forms are the foundation of life — that the cosmos itself brought forth life and human intelligence and that science, nature, and religion (I prefer spirituality — religion, as Tom Robbins puts it, is an inadequate response to the divine) are but different descriptions, different stories of the biosphere's troubled metamorphosis to consciousness and self-awareness.

It is here at its outer reaches that we can discover the principle that lies behind the law. Since there is already a Peter Principle and an Uncertainty Principle, I am left with no choice but to call it Brock's Principle. Brock's Principle states that full description includes the known, *plus* the unknown, *plus* the numinous. Three elements are required: what is known, *plus* what is as yet unknown but knowable, *plus* what is unknowable. This leaves us in a bit of a quandary because it becomes evident that even full description is impossible — let alone explanation.

It seems also to make the case that *story* is the only way to encompass life. And it brings us into direct confrontation with a culture based upon a hierarchy of explainers who reject two parts of the equation and take the first to be all three.

With Pepsi generation problems it is rather fun to find solutions coming from outside their definition. As we probe deeper we find that defining a problem by an arbitrary selection of what we know can bring surprises and that even integrating all we do know leaves the question incompletely defined or stalemated. It is seldom what we know as information that is used to solve problems anyway, but *how* we handle what is unknown (or unacknowledged) and what cannot be known. And here belief enters again. If our belief cannot stretch beyond a mere amalgam of the "factoids" we think we know, every question, large or small, will stumble and falter before the law.

Brock's Law applies forcefully and negatively, even fatally, when we insist upon keeping things separate and search for answers and act only where we find the questions. It is a trap for arrogance and though I first thought of it as a joke, it is a trickster's joke. And the joke is on us for we are all always enclosed in a cocoon of our own making.

On the other hand, the law can be helpful and positive when we acknowledge its truth and broaden our vision to include contexts and accept guidance from the cosmos. It is a hopeful law, a dynamic law, exciting to the human spirit's quest for deepening experience and adventure because it proclaims there are no boundaries and no limits to learning, no absolute answers or explanations, only new questions, new stories. It is indeed a law of life, for the only way to negate it is to achieve a perfect synthesis of body, mind, and spirit, a perfect unity of man and cosmos. Accepting the law helps you along that path.

The price of not understanding Brock's Law is that both Murphy's Law and the Peter Principle will hold: what can go wrong will and that we will be incompetent to deal with it.

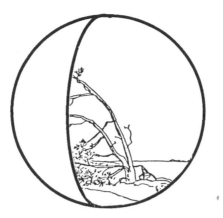

Brock's Law Revisited

What kind of a law suggests there are no laws? It's rather like a New Year's resolution which resolves to not make any New Year's resolutions. Brock's Law revisited seems only to reflect the apparent tendency of evolution to transcend, in an unpredictable way, what has gone before. It is therefore more in the nature of an observation than a law but law sounds authoritative, weighty, legitimate, powerful.

The best way to revisit Brock's observation is to get a laugh out of it.

In most cases a change of context is seen as threatening, as fearful, and it is this fear which often makes understanding and accepting the law difficult. But humour is exactly that — changing contexts.

Two Cockneys were wandering the streets of London when they came upon a wedding party leaving a church. An arch had been formed by eight men with oars under which the bride, the cox of the Cambridge rowing eight, and the groom stood waving at the guests. One Cockney turned to the other and said "Cor' look at all them oars." "Them's not 'ores" the other replied, "them's bridesmaids." Genuine humour is a change of context in which we all take great delight. It is the basis of humour all over the world and without it you can never understand the law!

If a problem is serious, does getting serious help? That may seem a curious question in these time of great seriousness, when there is so little evidence of humour around. But with everything so very serious it is perhaps time to loosen up. There is a firm connection between humour and intuition — they have the same root of instantly changing contexts.

Many inventions are the result of play and playfulness and it is often the case that answers come when you least expect them: when running, when in the bath like Archimedes, even when asleep. It seems then that we must allow contexts to swirl around as freely as they do in humour, allow our minds to be as hospitable to intuition as it is to humour. We work against it by taking our work, our dilemmas, our problems, and ourselves too seriously. So to get the best out of Brock's Law you need a sense of humour. Those who laugh — last!

The fanciful side of great thinkers is seldom portrayed. There is an essential element of playfulness in great scientific shifts. Creative and innovative thinkers revel in unsolved problems and play with their imaginations like children do with toys. Einstein imagined himself riding on a beam of light and this image led to the theory of relativity. Play can be said to be more important than playing it safe.

"Creative intellects are at peace with what they do not know. They are willing not to understand. You can't be intuitive if you're trying to be right," said Peter Senge of MIT's Systems Dynamics Group. We assume that cause and effect are directly linked but often they are not. That's another way to state the law.

It is helpful to remember the evolutionary concept stressed throughout these thoughts: one level depends upon and includes the ones below, though it transcends them, and none are predictable or explainable from the lower level. Well-structured, orderly work cannot be blithely skipped in order to acquire a hoped-for revelation. It feeds the mind. Henri Poincare suggests, "These efforts are not as sterile as one thinks; they set agoing the unconscious machine and without them it would not have moved and would have produced nothing." A period of incubation is necessary but based upon the hard work of preparation. Mozart, in talking of his music, said, "Whence and how it comes I know not, nor can I force it." The work must be done but not only the work.

In our education and training we take the look-before-you-leap dictum to absurd extremes where it becomes "psychosclerosis." It inhibits solutions, as does the obsessive need for order, the compulsion to do things by the book, and the demand for a quick solution. That is a sure way to be trapped by the law. Decision making and problem solving are usually portrayed as a straight line made up of formal, rational, steps, each one taken after we are certain of the previous step. This happens more often than we care to admit, and is no more than a way of rationalizing an already conceived goal but it appears very weighty, earnest and professional.

"Science is what you do after you guess well," said the great mathematician, Leonhard Euler. Science appears weighty and earnest too but it is the guessing which is important. One has to step out of rational habit and linear thinking to see the world differently.

John Sculley, creator of the Pepsi Generation slogan, discovered Brock's Law in his own way after much weighty and expensive rationalizing. Part of the reason there are so few good marketers, he seems to say, is that the discipline has been falsely chasing the god of science, when it is really an art. "Market analysis, to take one false god, tends to look at trends. There was no trend that led from the railway to the airplane, the horse and buggy to the car, ditto machine to Xerox, mainframe to personal computer," he writes. Pretty powerful insights for sugared water. But just wait.

Sculley, in my reading of him, goes further and says that usually you can only nullify a competitor's strength by changing the ground rules of the competition, not simply meeting the competitor on the same field with their rules. Too many marketers attempt to play within the existing competitive framework. Against Coke or IBM, that is a losing strategy. Coke, for instance, owned the world's most distinctive trademarks in its 6.5-ounce bottle. It was as American as apple pie.

Taste tests had convinced Pepsi that people preferred Pepsi if they didn't know beforehand which was which, so they were convinced that the market advantage was the bottle. Pepsi spent millions in new design studies and became so obsessed with new bottles and its competitor that it lost its perspective on the market.

Seeking to change the ground rules, Sculley initiated a massive consumer study in which he gave unlimited amounts of Pepsi to a study group and discovered that however much they took home they consumed it all. At that time the only way to buy soft drinks was in the small bottles or six packs. Instead of redesigning the standard bottles it became obvious that "we should change the rules" and launch larger and more varied packages. The market opportunity was not in shape but size. It wasn't until he shifted the ground rules to larger bottles that the market advantage to Coke with its distinctive bottle began to erode. The rest is history. Coke could not translate its distinctive bottle to a larger size. As a result, a trademark familiar to America for three generations became virtually extinct, became history! Whew, what a "go round."

In 1960, in a situation somewhat the reverse of Pepsi, people complained that Heinz ketchup was harder to pour than the competitors. Launching the "slowest pouring ketchup" theme ("richer, thicker, therefore tastes better etc.") they increased market share from 17 to 50 per cent. The company turned what had been seen as a disadvantage into a competitive advantage by changing the ground rules.

Imagine spending all that money, energy and creativity on these capitalist preoccupations. While not of the stature of Niels Bohr's complementarity, or even mainframes and personal computers, they show Brock's Law to be operative even at the lowest levels of daily existence.

Speaking of mainframes, the story doesn't end there. IBM would not admit there was any market at all for personal computers until long after Steve Jobs and the Woz came along with

Apple. Jobs was later convinced he wanted John Sculley, who now seemed to be bored with Pepsi, to take over Apple. He asked Sculley, "Do you want to spend the rest of your life selling sugared water or do you want a chance to change the world?" Evidently Sculley wanted to change the world and accepted the position as CEO of Apple. That solved Sculley's problems, since by then Coke and Pepsi were again playing the same game, but not Jobs'. Jobs was eventually fired by Sculley from the company he himself founded. And now Apple, under Sculley, has joined forces with IBM. Will we end up with big blue apples?

And what's next for Jobs? Personal mainframes maybe? And yet *The Economist* says there has been no increase in labour efficiency attributable to the enormous increase in computer purchases. Whatever now? People perhaps? This is all very weighty and earnest but you must admit it's funny.

Capitalism itself is a sure bet for Brock's Law to apply. As Ted Turner of CNN puts it, "You just go on growing until the government stops you." That of course admits to an external control — solutions to problems created by capitalism will come from elsewhere. Any system based upon subsidies and solutions from elsewhere is bound to fail according to the law. Capitalism has so far shown no aptitude for imitating natural systems and calling it sustainable doesn't help. Sustainable exploitation is an oxymoron where the last part of the word seems to apply.

One of the most interesting and pervasive corollaries of the law has to do with solutions which are appropriate in one context but which, when the context changes, or is not acknowledged in the first place, makes the solution the problem. We seem to hold on to things long past their usefulness, a reflection perhaps of our attempt to make the world static and linear, to make it safe, not admitting that it is inexorably dynamic. This is extraordinarily insidious and one of the most common conditions of man.

The Haida Indians in British Columbia once lived in a prodigiously productive environment which was nevertheless somewhat erratic. The salmon resource, though huge, was not universal to all who lived along the coast. Survival on the northwest coast depended very heavily upon co-operative effort. Harvesting timber or salmon could not be done alone. Social groups tended to be large enough to provide adequate labour at all times. Though the resources ostensibly belonged to a few families and chiefs, the potlatch, in effect, regulated the affairs of the villages. It was one of the ways status and stability was maintained by the chiefs but potlatch means gift or more precisely "a gift with an elastic attached so it will come back." Chiefs gave away their wealth — expecting to get it back of course. It was conspicuous sharing. There was no prestige in conspicuous consumption until the white man came.

Along with its obvious social function of defining resource ownership, establishing rank hierarchies, and maintaining bonds between individuals and groups, the pre-white-contact potlatch also served the very important function of encouraging production and then distributing the surplus more broadly than would otherwise have been the case. This was entirely appropriate and a valid survival strategy when the resources were their own local renewable resources and the system a relatively closed one. Social relations were determined by the potlatch while numbers and ambitions were tempered by the environment. It was a good adaptive strategy that grew out of giving and living in a fluctuating though limited world.

The fur trade changed all that when a society based upon taking and accumulating came upon one based upon giving and sharing. Goods previously circulated within it then poured out of the system to satisfy the demands of a quite foreign economy. Attempts to restore the stability, the lineage and the culture (which epidemics had also helped destroy), became a perversion of the original context. No longer tied to the resource base by the need to sustain large numbers of people on a fluctuating base, no longer entirely dependent upon a closed system, the potlatch became an example of what can happen to cultural strategies when their context is distorted and changed. Thousands of blankets, bags of flour, sides of salmon, and gallons of oil, were given away or more often destroyed. The post-contact potlatch, while no doubt a fascinating affair, became a bizarre aberration.

There are many lessons here, not least the effects of stretching a resource beyond its limit. It is particularly appropriate now that we realize that we live in a closed, though global, community. The magnificent system developed by the early Haida and other tribes firmly illustrates the law that a valid solution in one context becomes a problem in another.

In New Guinea to this day the men practise a similar tradition that had valid beginnings but has become a horror of maladaptive behaviour. Pigs are the most useful source of animal protein ever domesticated. They are a wonderful way to store surplus garden production. The only trouble with them is you have to eat them to cash in. They do not produce anything else except perhaps a few truffles. So in New Guinea the pigs grew and each year all but the breeding stock were slaughtered and eaten in a grand feast. Men cleared the land, started the gardens, the women worked the gardens that fed the people, and the pigs consumed the surplus and were shared. So far so good. It all seems OK at that stage. Not the greatest perhaps but it worked.

But pigs became a form of wealth which could be traded, and so created the "big men" who came to run the community. The establishment of the "big men" was the culmination of swidden agriculture which determined the social organization of the Papua, New Guinea highlands. With pigs, men bought wives who worked the land to produce the crops which fed the pigs which made the men wealthy in the eyes of other men. But the demand to feed more and more pigs increased so that the "big men" could get "bigger." Sound familiar? Sweet potatoes, once only 20 percent of women's gardens, became up to 60 percent. Pig food came to replace the human staple Taro as the basic crop.

The ceremony used to give away wealth, *Moka*, now culminates in a giant festival where thousands of pigs are slaughtered and eaten. People have died from eating too much and the pork has to be carved under water because of the stink. But it does get eaten, rotten or not, because it is by definition "a good thing." And the women and children who grow the sweet potatoes are undernourished because 60 percent of their production now goes to feed pigs reared for *moka* and the "big men."

Whereas pigs and wealth were once simply the surplus of good productive management, in the modern era they have become the primary requirement, serving not as food reserves but as the principle element in exchanges of wealth and in the "fantastic adornments and extravagant rituals" that serve only to bolster the prestige of the "big men." This one grew all on its own to become a parody of its beginnings.

But we should not be too smug about these examples of 'primitive' peoples. One could easily use the terms "fantastic adornments and extravagant rituals" as well as conspicuous consumption to define our own society. Adam Smith's capitalism, our own holy of holys, provides another example of the same thing. At the time he developed his ideas, society was "God fearing" and had a firm value system which he didn't think twice about. It was his culture. He is widely seen as the intellectual champion of self-interest but this is a misconception. Smith saw no moral virtue in selfishness; on the contrary, he saw its dangers. Still less was he a defender of capital over labour, or of the rising bourgeoisie over common folk. One of his most famous remarks tells the tale: "People of the same trade seldom meet together, even for merriment and diversion, but the conversation ends in a conspiracy against the public, or in some contrivance to raise prices." Far from praising self-interest as a virtue, he merely observed it could be a driving economic force and explained how a potentially destructive impulse, for he clearly saw its destructiveness, could be harnessed for social good. His idea was not meant to replace his values but to operate within them. It never occurred to him that self-interest itself would become the value system.

I remember an outburst of mine as a teenager which was more insightful than I then knew. I argued once, perhaps even shouted, that capitalism depended upon the Christian ethic being held by most people, but not by all. I did not know then the conditions of its creation, and we have indeed forgotten them, but it is obvious now that the context has changed and that capitalism obeys Brock's Law. It has grown beyond its adaptive value and the unrecognized conditions of its creation. There is no question that it works magnificently as a means of producing surplus but it is no more relevant, in a changed context, than producing rotten pork or burning Hudson's Bay blankets. It is no longer a question of more pigs or more blankets.

Capitalism has moved beyond its adaptive survival strategy and become a parody of itself and perhaps its own antithesis. The solutions will be found outside the narrow contexts of its present focus. This has not yet been recognized. We simply think we have to make it work better, that to get out of our present hot water we should not just sit there but "go out and buy something." Pitifully it has become as irrelevant and destructive as the New Guinea pigs!

A point can be made about our all too common tendency to resist acknowledging Brock's Law. It is obvious in the case of the Haida and "the big men" of New Guinea that change can be left so long that serious suffering and dislocation result. Indeed, it seems historically that change is not possible from within but only collapse. A famous but gruesome frog story rings true. Put a frog in hot water and it will jump out. Put it in cold water and then heat the water and you will have a cooked frog.

An honest look at capitalism, at the moment thought of as the winner over socialism, indicates dangers are approaching quickly. The water is approaching boiling point. With atoms, with molecules, with cells, and in communities of cells or people, change takes place at the boundaries. Solutions come from outside the established order preceded only by a lot of furious and impotent tinkering at the centre. Brock's Law is really about recognizing and expanding boundaries and contexts. The primary context is the functioning of the earth and any solution which does not take that fact as its very basis is doomed to obey the law's worst prediction — that what can go wrong will and that we will be incompetent to deal with it.

Focusing on capitalism or socialism leaves consumerism, the avowed aim of both, unexamined and we easily become trapped by the law. Neither is relevant to the problems found within them and both are, at their base, but different ways of trying to do the same thing. And both are trying to cope with an unadmitted or unrecognized change of context.

One-fifth of the world's population lives in 'developed' economies. Now that capitalism has won, is its task to bring the remaining four-fifths to the same level? The planet will have something to say about that. Seventy-five years of 'development' by one-fifth of its population has left the future of the other four-fifths and of the planet itself in serious doubt. This is now cautiously admitted — but its cause denied — even by the 'developed' one-fifth. Perhaps this is the case of a solution becoming the problem when the context changes.

In spite of my earlier pronouncement it is hard to laugh. On the other hand it is hard not to laugh. If you were suddenly put into this cauldron of competition, conspicuous consumption and fantastic adornments you would jump right out and call it insane. And some poor macho frog would call out to you, "Hey! If you can't stand the heat get out of the kitchennnnnn!"

Getting Home

Khudo, or meditation khudo, is Japanese archery, a formal practice with prescribed and coordinated moves — a ceremony where the proper release of the arrow is the target, not the target itself. All the time I was watching a demonstration recently I was for some reason thinking about haymaking. The way the mental approach was described and the intense concentration seemed to remind me of building a stack of loose hay, or building a wagon load of bales alone in the field. It struck me at first as a peculiar thought.

Haymaking and khudo both require coordination and complete "mindfulness." There is a prescribed pattern for building a haystack but it is as loose and free as the hay itself. There are moves that work which are as graceful and elegant as those of khudo. Perhaps the archers who devote so much time to their practice have never built a haystack. It seems to me to hold the same promise though without the heritage or formalism. Perhaps a good day in the field would bring as much satisfaction if it was approached the same way — with reverence and focused upon the spirit of the thing. And how else should one approach the planet?

Khudo's purpose is to discover "one's basic goodness." But in relation to what? A bow? An arrow? A target? No — these are but the path. And why, if it takes ten years to learn to hold a bow a certain way and the practice is more than 500 years old, is it more significant than learning how to hold and use a pitchfork? The pitchfork is certainly more useful and I can assure you that one needs to be supremely "mindful" strenuously wielding a fork one-quarter inch from the unseen ground. If shooting an arrow can lead to a deep personal experience why not making hay, or catching fish, or harvesting a woodlot? In each case, I think, it depends entirely upon how you go about it.

I have been interested in Bhuddist thought since wading through some of *The Golden Bough* as a young man searching for relief from the preposterous idea that I was, even that I had been born, a sinner. Imagine coming across the idea of basic goodness — that goodness and the path to the sacred could be found within. It has supported and enriched my relationship with the planet ever since, though an intimate and comforting sense of oneness has been dominant.

My interest in Buddhist thought and practice grew and recently I took a level one session in sitting meditation called Shambala training. The practice arose out of Tibetan Bhuddist tradition and the wisdom and generosity of Chogyam Trungpa, who introduced it to the West without the trappings of Bhuddist ceremony. It is devoted to fostering self-awareness and is very simple. The philosophy matches my own since I believe there is an evolutionary imperative which leads us to reflective self awareness as a level above consciousness.

This involves sitting comfortably with your eyes open, allowing inevitable thoughts, feelings, ideas to wash through you, not denying them but labelling them *thinking* and letting them pass. There is no sense of getting into a trance but indeed of the opposite, of achieving heightened awareness. Your discipline is in labelling your thoughts *thinking* and letting them go on your out-breath. That's it. Sitting acknowledges its own artificial nature but you end up confronting yourself and this *inner work*, as writer Schumacher calls it, is the first step to an awareness which goes beyond the self.

Again a curious thought came to me. In trying to find a comfortable position I found myself sitting as I do when I paddle a canoe. I was then able to sit through the whole day without discomfort. Then, in a variation, we found ourselves practising walking meditation, concentrating on each step, the placing of the foot, the undefined awareness of the act. It hit me again. That is the only way to carry an 80-pound canoe for two miles. Wow! Meditation canoe tripping.

I thought back to my days in the woods. Paddling, when done day by day, becomes as automatic as breathing and each push at the end of a stroke is a thing to concentrate on, to release. One is virtually in the same state except for the sparkling water, the wind always, it seems, in your face, the next headland approaching with almost painful slowness. What one does is let one's thoughts wash through, allow them passage, and keep paddling to the next portage. If it is a long one you use the same technique of being aware of the act, gently shifting the weight of the canoe from one shoulder to the other or from the shoulders to the forehead and the tump-line. I had been practising meditation before I even knew the word. But there was a difference; I feel a significant difference. It was active and took place intimately and directly connected to the planet. It did not just seek, it was a oneness, an awareness of the sun and the whistling pines, the sharp golden V of a swimming beaver in the evening light, the rising mist of early mornings, the soft warm rains and yes, up to a point, the mosquitoes. Welcome them, let them be. They are you, too. It is all you.

To me there is a curious sense of being apart from the planet in practices like sitting meditation and "mind archery," that seems to leave them insipid and incomplete. They are urban and elitist, in the sense of being removed from the planet. Their origins tell the tale — the monk sitting on his high perch supported by the peasants below, the arrow, an instrument of war made obsolete by gunpowder, used in a new way. The attitudes learned in khudo or sitting meditation are enormously relevant to living on the planet, but I feel they struggle to connect without being connected.

"Walking is the great adventure, the first meditation, a practice of heartiness and soul primary to the human kind. The exact balance of spirit and humility," writes Gary Snyder. "To be well educated is to have learned the songs, proverbs, stories, myths and technologies that come from this experiencing of the non-human planet. Practice in the field, in open country, is foremost." Is he not closer in open country to the substance, to the essence which created these practices than are the rituals of sitting silent in a room or with great formality releasing an arrow at a target that doesn't matter? Bruce Chatwin declares that we have a built-in imperative to travel, that our large brain is for "singing our way through the wilderness."

Europeans were becoming nature illiterate as early as the sixteenth century. Major blocks of citified mythology denied first the soul, then consciousness, and finally even sentience to the natural world. Huge numbers of Europeans, in the climate of a nature-denying mechanistic ideology, were losing the opportunity for direct experience of nature. "By way of a trade-off they learned human management, administration, and rhetoric" — to paraphrase Snyder again. And the monk withdrew to his cave to practise meditation long before that. We have only recently begun to recognize the consequences to the planet of these attitudes of mind abstracted from the direct activity of living on the earth.

We have lost great swaths of land, destroyed vast forests, dragged and bulldozed ocean bottoms — the neighbourhood of fishes — and there is little recognition that in doing so we diminish not only ourselves but also the opportunity to practise mind haymaking, meditative fishing, and profound forestry. And why not? We see them as dull and mindless work, we city-folk. We assign them to the lower level of human activity as does the monk walled into his cave and fed through a hole while immersed in his higher calling, or the chairman unwittingly planning strategies to destroy the world. But they can be the opposite; they can be the highest calling and a path to real connectedness. To say nothing now of mere survival.

There is something of both the bhodisattva and the pragmatist in this sense, for we can all find in ourselves the higher awareness which earth processes have created — in activity directly connected to the processes themselves. Ceremony, certainly, transcendent awareness, certainly — it may be possible for us all. But begin where we began. I do not deny the monk his enlightenment, nor his practice, nor his search. But he needs the support not just of the peasants but of the earth. If the Buddhist vow of enlightenment "for the sake of all living things" is to mean anything, let us not forget those who work with living things, let us not forget those who till the soil or harvest the oceans. Indeed, let us begin there. Begin with the earth.

Walled in his cave or isolated in our own separate cocoons amounts to a denial of life. The business of living, of making a living on the planet, is a sacred activity if you believe the planet to be sacred. We must live upon the earth, must harvest and build. If we can use the attitudes learned in khudo and sitting meditation, reinvent them and bring them to the earth, then perhaps we can find that a way to feel connected is by *being* connected. Perhaps we can discover our "basic goodness" in the very act of participating in and maintaining the basis of our own life.

Seekers create prophets, as has been written elsewhere. What is this need to raise a person to such stature? When the *sawang*, a leader of the Bhuddist church, comes to town he is driven in limousines, given alms, and he is served. It is said he does not notice, does not even see *mistakes* in the serving practice when he is served. The serving then must satisfy something in the server. An acquaintance claims to feel more "alive" when serving, perhaps like Thelma did when she began robbing stores in *Thelma and Louise*. The *sawang* no doubt sees himself as a symbol of a "greater being," if he thinks about it that way at all. Others, the seekers, in their need to feel alive when serving him, perhaps confuse the symbol for the substance, the map for the terrain.

And if we seek perfection we will not, except by denial, find it there. No man deserves that kind of reverence which I feel, in a curious way, diminishes him. But the planet does. Serving a man or an ideology, even as a symbol, in some slightly perverse way, forfeits and blinds us to the vitality that serving and celebrating the planet can bring.

These attitudes and postures of old cultures, Christian or Buddhist, can be enlarged to serve and revere the reality of the planet. Admiration, emulation of the prophet's goodness, wisdom, or service — yes indeed. Mother Theresa would be the first to agree with "Do as I do," though she would be the last to say it. But why stop with Christ, with the Buddha, with the *sawang*? They themselves claim only to be the path, only to show the way. To serve them denies their teaching.

Perhaps it is loneliness, isolation, the sense of aloneness, of separateness which creates this need for prophets, for fathers. We are removed from the processes of life which is where our devotion and our reverence can lie and which, at the same time, can temper the loneliness. And if we need symbols, is not each tree a symbol? Is not a tree, a fish, a blade of grass both the reality and the symbol of the processes which created it? I look now at leaves outside my window. Try to imagine another way to capture sunlight so that each plant, each leaf may gain. Look at how they fill the space but at the same time leave room. An intricate blanket tuned to the sun's motion, at once unity and diversity, autonomy and mutual dependence, a manifestation and a symbol of life.

There is perfection. And there perhaps is the place for both action and worship, beyond ceremony or mind or shrine rooms, beyond prophets, in the activity of living and being. There perhaps is a way home, the way to reinhabit the earth.

"Good — but not Good Enough"

L earning has been given a bum rap. It's generally thought to be what you do in school, and that's generally thought to be the kind of passive absorption of knowledge from experts which we all know about only too well. In a limited sense this is true and that kind of learning can be called maintenance or adaptive learning. It's like punching data into a computer and punching seems an appropriate word. It's what you do to keep up. You accumulate knowledge and know-how, and if you're good at it you might become a know-it-all. But you're still behind. Those who follow are always behind.

This kind of learning, in school and at work, is not the whole story by any means. It is necessary of course, and was, until recently, all we thought was necessary. But it is a trap. The world has changed, and the events of the past decade — or even the past day — can hardly leave a doubt in anyone's mind. The world is not as mechanistic and as subject to our control as we pretend. Learning is not passive linear processing of static data, though we have made it so, but active, dynamic, infinitely complex, creative and unpredictable. So is the earth.

In the past, the way we have gone about learning — both process and content — has created many of the problems we now face. One hundred years ago schools were broadly introduced to teach literacy; instruction was and remains the focus. A history of swings in methods and approach based on little more than changing fashions and politics has merely grown new wrinkles on an old face. And more, static, separate, often obsolete, usually biased knowledge has just added more hay to the same old wagon lurching down the same old rutted road. And hay it is — desiccated, poorly preserved and becoming mouldy, cut while growing but with little left of life or vitality. The metaphor is appropriate. Hay, as any farmer knows, maintains life until new growth comes and schools are barns where maintenance rations are stored and fed in a way arranged for the convenience of those who do the feeding. An image that I have seen many times comes to me: it is of cattle kept in stalls, chained by the neck, fed and mucked out, mangy and listless — all for the sake of the farmer. The stock grows restless or pines away, kept from their pastures, awaiting life to begin anew.

Einstein once said, "It is, in fact, nothing short of a miracle that modern methods of instruction have not entirely strangled the holy curiosity of inquiry; for this delicate little plant, aside from stimulation, stands mainly in need of freedom."

This "holy curiosity" is the lightning rod for innovation and learning and works best when the mind is unpressed and genuinely animated by intrinsic desire. But from the earliest grades we penalize errors, even reprimand pupils who offer up guesses, half-formed feelings and vague hunches. This behaviour tells students that it doesn't pay to take risks and they become mistrustful of thoughts that are not exactly what the teacher wants. They learn to play it safe and dismiss the very things that frequently lead, with practice, to discovery and learning. The very things that give new life.

In education, we imagine that there are such things as teachers and get very focused upon the word. But there are no teachers, only people who create opportunities for learning. And by far the most common method of teaching is the least effective in creating these opportunities: recital by an "expert" of facts and the display of finished products. It is worse than being ineffective. It is harmful. Do not imagine for a minute pupils do not recognize the sham. Learning by definition is an activity, the creation of one's own reality. Learners already have a huge amount of experience before they even get to school.

One teaches what one is far more than what one knows and what we call a teacher is first and foremost a model of how to use the mind. If one could be seen making guesses, running up blind alleys and chasing fugitive hunches, indeed being human, one's own uncertain intuitions and meanderings would gain legitimacy. This would require demonstrated inquisitiveness and joy in discovery and being seen to be unafraid to make mistakes. A tall order perhaps to become a person, not just a dispenser of data, to sacrifice the expert status and give up power to empower others, but the pretence that we know what we're doing doesn't wash any more.

Expert is a double downer, both put down and close down — put down for others and close down for the expert. A friend who has thought deeply about this suggests the bifurcation point comes when one truly knows that one can learn from one's students, which is pretty close to the opposite of the present situation. And it can be put in a different way. The difference is the shift between explainer and describer. An explainer says, "Let me tell you the way it is." But ultimately one confronts the mystery and realizes there are no explanations and the posture becomes untenable. Explanations are about power and control and need the support of half truths, half truths about what is being explained — and about the explainer. The 'data' can be often the same but a describer says, "Let me tell you a story," an attitude which recognizes the mystery and the subjective nature of knowledge and therefore acknowledges the validity of other knowledge and experience. These changes push at the very structure and purpose of schooling and a bold new vision of another road, and another wagon appears.

Business too has similar problems to ponder. Millions are spent retraining people whom schools train for an industrial job market which no longer exists. But beyond that there is mounting evidence that the entire industrial culture which spawned the business world no longer exists.

At a simple level, next to *profits* the word most associated with business is *management*. In the fifties and sixties problem solving was the "idiom" of management training, and for the most part still is. In a stable, growing economy it was sufficient as a journey along a familiar road to a known destination. Problem solving is still as vital as ever and no corporation can survive without it, but unfortunately it is no longer sufficient. Problem finding, and defining is a great deal more difficult and important than problem solving.

Corporate structure puts problem solving at one level and problem defining at another almost entirely separate level as though they were not even connected (in school they aren't). To quote deBono's "catch 24," "In order for a person to reach the most senior positions in an organization, he or she must have kept hidden — or not had — exactly those talents needed when he (she) gets there." Not surprisingly, the processes of gaining insight and understanding are quite different from those of gaining factual knowledge. Our attitudes towards learning as merely adaptive, in school or at work, affects the whole fabric of our world.

School and business have the same problem: what was good is no longer good enough. The game is no longer just more information or more stuff and the crisis is not one of efficiency but of imagination. It is a problem caused by not really believing the world is a dynamic, transforming community. What was is still necessary, just not enough. At the base we still need knowledge, we still need problem-solving skills, we still need at least some of the stuff the work world produces, but the new mode represents a quantum leap to another plane.

What has forced this upon us, indeed, demands that we understand, is not just change, but the increasing rate and scale of change. Adapting to gradual change is learning without realizing it — it is passive, reactive, and painless. Failure to adapt may result in learning by shock but at today's pace and scale the shock can be not just painful but fatal. One dimension of our need to become a learning society, a society based upon more than mere knowledge or of being more than mere consumers, is simply survival. And I do not mean survival in the world's marketplace. The worldwide panic to become competitive in one context is not an effective way to foster a new context.

The other dimension is far more interesting and exciting: the adventure of learning. Each of us has enormous potential, and many ways of knowing. It is nothing short of awe inspiring to witness the transformation of a person who realizes that he or she can learn and that learning, the spark that enlightens deeper understanding, is the most satisfying, challenging, and rewarding activity of life. This produces real motivation, not just rah, rah, up-the-company hype or trust-me-I'm-an-expert teaching, but self-initiated activity and creativity, a "choice to learn," a lifelong process of developing hidden or unknown potentialities.

Is that not how the earth has developed potentialities? And is it not a dynamic and ever transforming process? In our panic to survive we forget we are here, we are alive and of the earth, of the cosmos, that we are indeed transformed stardust. Darwin, who got almost everything wrong, is not a good guide. The earth has more experience. Evolution is a process of developing potentialities based upon dependent but transcendent change.

It is curious we have such problems with the idea. Atoms are "good" but not as "good" as molecules, which are not as "good" as cells. It is obvious that, as far as cells are concerned, molecules are good but not good enough and that cells are something which transcend mere molecules, miraculous in themselves though they are. Even rocks are more than a merely random collection of atoms.

Here, I think, is a guide to the process which confronts us all and it is process we must look to — mere facts like mere atoms are not good enough. If survival was all it was about, atoms seem perfectly adapted to survive. Indeed, an atom of oxygen contained in any breath breathed in the last few hundred years is almost certain to be contained in your next breath. You may breathe in some of Darwin's last breath — the same unaltered oxygen atom. Talk about survival. Oxygen seems pretty permanent to me but before there was oxygen, which incidentally was poisonous to life, or before there was iron there was only hydrogen, and before that there were not even any atoms! Something which transcends survival is going on here.

Darwin's impoverished view of life as mere adaptation is reflected in our own impoverished view that learning and working is merely adaptive. Earth processes develop potentialities and each of us can take learning and being to a new height which transcends but includes the mere accumulation of knowledge and stuff. Learning and living, like earth processes, are active, dynamic and creative — can develop potentialities. Now *there* is an adventure into the unknown.

It is useful to turn to E.F. Schumacher in his *Guide for the Perplexed*. He turns to Thomas Aquinas who says, "Knowing comes about insofar as the object known is within the knower." Schumacher writes about the "adequacy" of intellectual senses, of *the mind in action*. He suggests that the mind is adequate to know only what it can believe. We see not just with our senses but with our minds — believing is seeing.

This weekend we were clearing a trail along the edge of the sea moving   up to five hundred feet and down again through the yellow and red of an autumn forest above a surging ocean. It was hot work. At about lunch time, we came to a narrow path along a steep scree slope, turned a corner, and burst out of the woods to a view of the colour of far hills and a river valley. We stopped to sit a while. Schumacher's levels of knowing came to mind.

To some, indeed to most in this television age, it would be "magnificent scenery" or perhaps a dark foreboding forest — entertainment or fear. There were solid patches of dark spruce reaching down the hill to the sea. Forest still, or pasture spruce growing back to reclaim land once cultivated? To know that is to see differently. To have worked at clearing a trail is to know the land in another way and to know there were 200 Cape Breton families living there once is to hear the music of the fiddle and see the step dancing in the silence.

These were levels of knowing based upon information to be sure, but a mind which just sees forest is literally incapable of knowing there is anything else to see. There *is* nothing else to see. That mind, clever though it may be, is inadequate for more. If all you have is a hammer everything is nails. Clearly, information is the base but knowing goes beyond by transcending the facts.

Schumacher does not use belief in the sense of belief in Christ or democracy, of external belief, but belief at the deepest level of your being in what you are and can be. And as he puts it, "The level of significance of what is seen, or known, is chosen, not by intelligence, but by faith. If I lack faith and consequently choose an inadequate level of significance for an investigation, no degree of objectivity will save me from missing the point and I rob myself of the very possibility of understanding. Lacking belief I cannot see."

This was a problem Darwin was unacquainted with. Indeed, he chose, as have his followers to this day, to replace faith with facts, not realizing faith determines facts. It is tricky. "All knowledge is 'subjective' in as much as it cannot exist other than in the mind of a human subject." Schumacher again. Or as Nietzsche put it, "Let us, from now on, be on our guard against the hallowed philosopher's myth of a pure, willess, timeless knower. All seeing is essentially perspective and so is all knowing." Back to Aquinas — what is known is somehow "within the knower."

And back to sitting in the autumn sun. The rock I was sitting on was covered with lichen. To Darwin it was one of the oldest kinds of plant, adapted and well able to survive in hostile environments. But it is not exactly one plant; it is two autonomous organisms with their own DNA, their own metabolism, but mutually dependent and mutually supporting. Even its simplest molecules are more than atoms locked in random competition. And protein, of which there is perhaps none in lichen, contains 10,000 atoms with not one out of place. The earth has known this for a very long time. If your belief limits your world view to random chance and mere survival then that is what you will see and all you will know. No degree of "objectivity" will save you from missing the point. It is all you can know.

The cosmic process of developing potentialities has been relentless for fifteen billion years and no transcendent level has been predictable or knowable from its earlier base. Atoms reached the limit of their potential early on in the journey, then became the base for something entirely unknowable to atoms. We can barely glimpse, through a shroud of fear and inertia, our own possible potential. It is indeed frightening and unknowable. But passive absorption of secondhand data and merely doing well for ourselves is inadequate to take us there. We must embark upon a journey beyond mere adaptive survival and transform learning to more than knowing mere facts .

Someone once asked Steve Podborski what to do when skiing fast on ice. His answer: "Go for it." Curiously, that too may be our only route to survival. It is certainly the only way to survive on ice — the second you lose your nerve you're down. And maybe that is what it will take. The nerve to try to be fully human. The frontier stretches beyond survival, beyond consciousness, to reflective self-awareness, and to who knows, or can know, where. It is a potentiality we must strive for. It seems to be an evolutionary imperative that manifesting potential may be the best, perhaps the only, survival strategy. What potential did a dinosaur have beyond being just a dinosaur and merely surviving? Perhaps some of them became birds! Perhaps, to survive, we must aim beyond mere survival, strive to reach what is beyond our grasp and beyond our ken, allow our souls to fly. Perhaps only that is good enough.

A Silent Swerving

I guess you'll be going sailing again today."

Bonny and I were having breakfast in the early morning light. There was a soft breeze from the east and a clear sky — a sure sign that by about ten-thirty the wind would flop round to the west and begin to blow in earnest. We have two old Lasers and often sail together, one in each boat, but it was going to blow and she decided I should go alone.

Get into the shorty wet suit and boots, wrap up the nylon shell and pants, find a chocolate bar and an orange, glasses, a hat and lifejacket, rig the boat and it was off for the day. It was gentle to begin and I quietly weaved south through the outer fringe of islands to the open water.

Georgian Bay is a land of big sky and far horizons. It draws you to them and frees the mind. Not that one consciously or purposefully ponders big questions but rather is seduced out of the myopia of daily and mundane things. The landscape infects me and, combined with sailing, does it to me every time.

In 1924 G.K. Chesterton wrote, "The real trouble with this world of ours is not that it is an unreasonable world, or even that it is a reasonable one. The common kind of trouble is that it is nearly reasonable, but not quite. Life is not an illogicality, yet it is a trap for logicians. Considering the symmetry of the human body would lead us to expect two hearts. The world looks just a little more mathematical and regular than it is; its exactitude is obvious but its inexactitude is hidden, its wildness lies in waiting. Everywhere there is a silent swerving from accuracy by an inch that is the uncanny element in everything — a sort of secret treason in the universe." This is the perception of a writer of a past age and a past understanding. It is true except for the treason bit, for without that silent swerving he speaks of, without the dissymmetry, without the inexactitude, we would not exist — for evolution would be impossible. We are at a bifurcation point now between the classical and an evolving modern view, between the search for symmetry, for order, for predictability as the basis of the universe, and the recognition that chaos is an essential component of a dynamic universe. Symmetry and order are obvious in our being but not in our becoming and the universe is both. The growing perception is that order arises out of chaos, and indeed that nothing is constant but process and that process depends upon a "silent swerving" from perfect order. Far from being treasonous it is the life force of the universe.

As I worked my way south, my anticipation of the wildness lying in waiting grew because the wind was building, as predicted. Far on the horizon, faintly visible as shimmering vertical lines, a group of islands, the Watchers, which I had never reached, was twelve miles away and five miles off shore. They beckoned but the angle was a bit tight and I settled for an easier tack to the Pine Islands slightly closer and closer to the mainland.

From the very beginning, there was an unbalance matched by exquisite exactitude. The force which began the expansion of the universe had to be absolutely precise. Too little or too much and it would have quickly collapsed or cosmic matter would have been entirely frozen. The rate of expansion had to be exactly right to allow for the supercooling responsible for the onset of disequilibrium. It had to be perfect to be imperfect! As Hubert Reeves puts it in his book *The Hour of our Delight*, "The history of the universe is not characterized by the disintegration of an initial strongly organized order; on the contrary it is the story of the construction over eons of a pyramid of complexity. Astronomy, physics, chemistry, and biology reveal it in all its splendour. By causing phases of disequilibrium, expansion introduces irreversibility and the unprecedented, and, as a result, enables the growth of complexity and variety on a cosmic scale." It is the fertility of disequilibrium which creates diversity and the unprecedented and which creates the observer to observe it. But not too much or too little. We have had narrow escapes from the sterility of perfect order or absolute chaos from the very beginning.

Hubert Reeves, a Canadian living in Paris, is one of the world's leading theoretical physicists. Convention has set him at an opposite pole but he has arrived at the same point as Tom Berry. Or perhaps, to get another little dig in for Brock's Law, it is better to say they have both fused and transcended their poles. Reeves spent a lot of time at sea under the stars as a young man and would appreciate my growing delight as the wind picked up. Delight is a word he uses. I was by now hiked out with my feet hooked under the hiking strap, the board half up and humming. That's the sign when the centre board starts to hum. We were moving now, old 10110 and I, a dance of tiller, weight, sail and wind. The Pine Islands arrived far sooner than I expected. Ten miles had gone by in a dream. The wind was steady but had moved further west. The Watchers were possible today. Go for it. I stopped for an orange by just letting the sail out and then hauled it in again and we were off. Bring on the unprecedented, bring on disequilibrium, bring on the irreversible — big words for a small sailing adventure but what the hell. That was the basis of my delight too and adventure is adventure.

Disequilibrium and the unprecedented can be brought closer to daily life. Recently Gwynne Dyer, an historian of war, gave a talk and spoke of the three years that saw the end of the Cold War as a time without precedent in human history. Dramatic changes, he says, have taken place in the world order without destructive violence, meaning *war*. As he himself suggests, if he had tried to predict the changes before they had happened, which he admits he could not have done, he would have been "bundled off to the luny bin." He suggested that there have been massive and unpredictable changes before but they have always been accompanied by violence, that there are long periods of stability and then short periods of great fluidity during which dramatic change takes place. Hidden in his analysis of this unprecedented sudden peaceful change is the observation that change happens quickly and unpredictably. Darwin notwithstanding, this pattern of quiet stability and sudden change is in fact the norm over the last fifteen billion years.

Darwin's greatest obsession was that change happened gradually, not *per saltum*, not in jumps. He would not let go of the idea that gradual change was the norm, that it was the pattern of all history. His thesis was unsupported by any evidence whatsoever and his writing seems to me to be but a massive attempt to convince himself. During the last one hundred years when the suggested evidence would come to light it has, without exception, all been against him. Darwin even denied his own experience for he had had a sudden insight early in life which changed instantly and forever his own thinking. The pattern of history is one of sudden and unpredictable transcendent change.

Someone in the audience asked Dyer if history was no longer a means of predicting the future, which he suggested was its purpose. Was this the end of history? Dyer, himself a former historian as he put it, gently said it was certainly no longer as useful. The person who asked the question was, perhaps unknowingly, a Darwinian or a Victorian; they amount to the same thing, for implicit in his question was the gradual linear progress they were all so stuck on.

The failed coup d'état in Moscow in 1991 finally deleted the Marxist definition of history as a system of linear projection and averaging data. As much an article of faith in the capitalist West as in the socialist East, predictive history has at last been exposed as an ideological abstraction. History, like science, cannot handle the unprecedented, the silent swerving.

Gradual change is a chimera. Piaget's thought on how children learn points to disequilibrium at the base. Thomas Kuhn illuminates scientific revolution by the same light. Learning is creating yourself by means of the unprecedented. So with the planet. And so too the need for the "silent swerving."

Time for a chocolate bar. I was watching the cormorants as I circled North Watcher Island. Now what? The wind had risen some more. It was about three o'clock and where I had to go now was no longer in sight. To get back meant a straight reach across open water five miles offshore. But the wind was exactly right, just over my shoulder, and the waves now about four feet. It was going to be some scoot home. It is all very well being drawn to the horizon but you have to get back too. On the other hand the alternative is to stay home.

In order to explore the reasons for the peaceful transformation he was speaking about, Dyer himself broadened and lengthened his horizon and suggested that the explanation could be understood as the beginning of the end of paternalist politics. And that this could be understood as a function of communication, of the "global brain," to use mathematician Peter Russell's term, establishing its synapses. Perhaps.

But if we broaden and lengthen the view even more and examine the evolution of the cosmos as history we may find some of the patterns we seek. To even imagine that human history is linear and can avail one of prediction only sets us up for surprises. "Although the study of [human] history resolves nothing," writes Lewis Lapham, "it offers the ceaseless example of man defining and then redefining the meaning of his existence." Perhaps it is indeed an end of the narrow history we know. But perhaps it can also be the beginning of a new and broader definition of history as a description of the cosmos. "The history of the universe is the central theme around which the various branches of knowledge can best be harmonized and give meaning," writes Hubert Reeves. "The temporal sequence of nuclear, atomic, molecular, and biological evolution links human existence to the very remote past and gives a deep reading of history." That is, the far horizon which draws us and gives us a secure place protected from the narrow propaganda we know now as history. I don't know about you but I say good riddance to the endless list of kings and tyrants, to smug and superficial explanations, to propaganda that is but a selected and self-serving record of the winners, to patterns of thought in the service of slogans, to history, and science, carried far beyond their legitimate role of description, used as tools for power and control.

The far horizon stretching back fifteen billion years gives us, and all life, firm roots in the very remote past. It is equally true that we must get back home to our own lives. Hubert Reeves, who seems to have been along on this adventure with me, puts it much better than I can: "Becoming adult means that, without too much pain, one can accept the idea that there is no Santa Claus. An adult learns to cope with doubt and uncertainty. Science cannot answer many questions but scientific knowledge does allow us to define our place in the cosmos in relation to stars, plants and animals. Science retraces our past, uncovers our cosmic roots, and describes the adventure of matter's organization of which our existence is a part.

"In order to live and interact with our fellow beings, each of us develops a personal philosophy of life, a personal world vision. It is in the elaboration of this world vision that scientific knowledge plays a primordial role. I am overcome by an irresistible surge of exaltation, gratitude and delight for life and the universe that engendered it."

Miriam McGillis has said, "The supreme crisis of our time is that we do not have a transforming vision of hope." True, we do not have static certainty, do not have predictability, not even stability for long, but perhaps some understanding that the cosmos is inexorably dynamic and that this is the germ of life can bring hope.

It took fifteen billion years of life for you to be able to think about this sentence. It was not possible sooner, nor was it possible in a smaller universe, nor was it possible in a sterile, ordered, or predictable universe. To recognize the "silent swerving" but to think of it as treasonous amounts to hopelessness and to a denial of life. To know it as the very basis of life gives meaning and hope to the wildness lying in waiting.

And it turned out that it was. As I buzzed along to the centreboards hum there was a new and deeper, a louder roar behind me which seemed to come from above the horizon. Looking back over my shoulder I saw a wave breaking far above me. I had no time to think about this unprecedented monster but instinctively threw myself back against it as it crashed over me. Poor old 10110 and I were completely submerged in the tumbling water, but we shuddered to the surface, amazingly still going in the same direction. The cockpit drained easily since the plug was out and we were soon planing again down the steep waves. The wave sure cleaned off my sunglasses.

It happened once more but the wind was dying now and my home island was in view. I literally fell out of the boat when I got back, exhausted by over six hours of hiking, but possessed by an incredible peace. Think about the words Hubert Reeves uses to describe the cosmos: *splendour, adventure, delight, exaltation, gratitude*. It had been that kind of day and it was time for tea.

Lines to See By

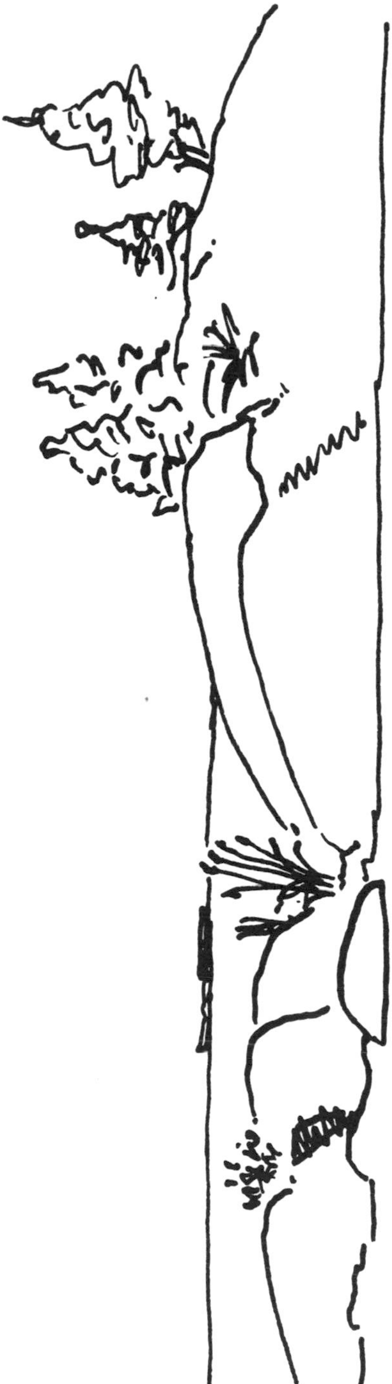

PWB

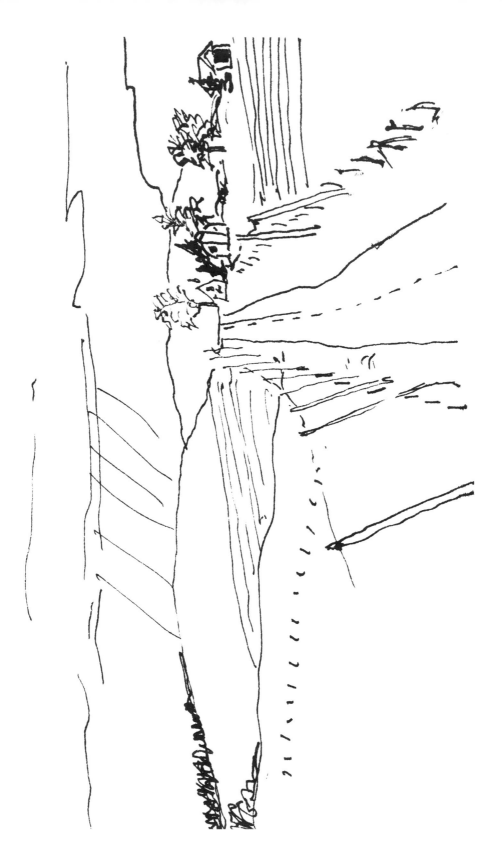

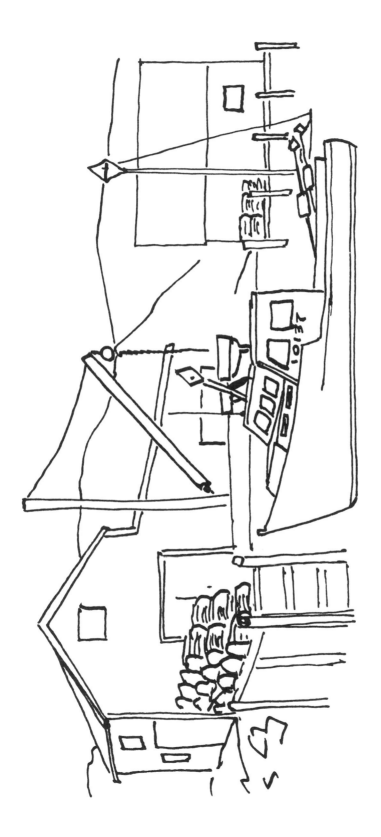

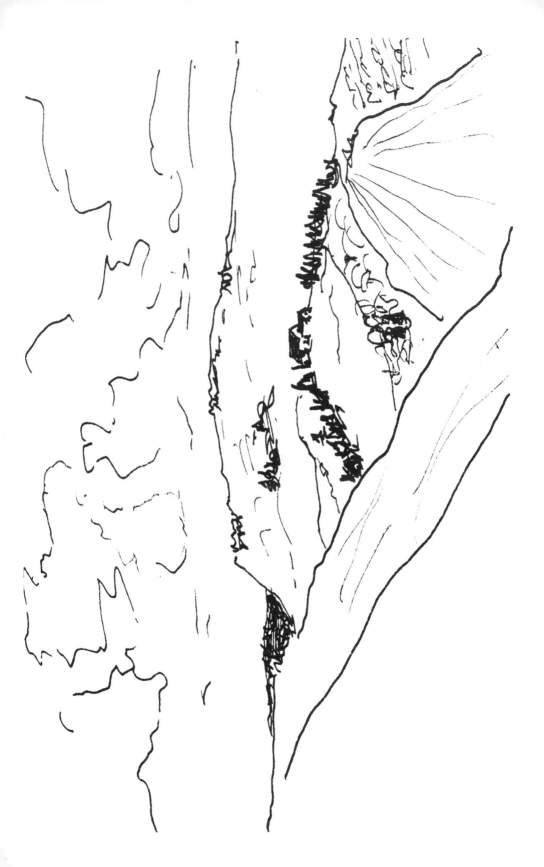

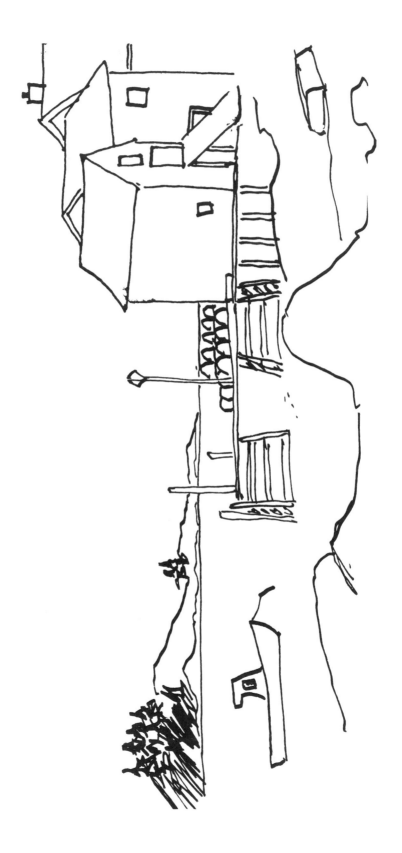

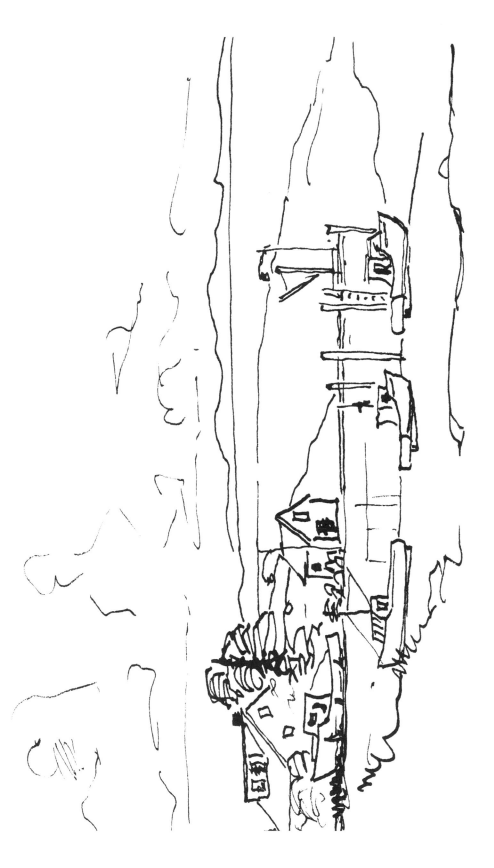

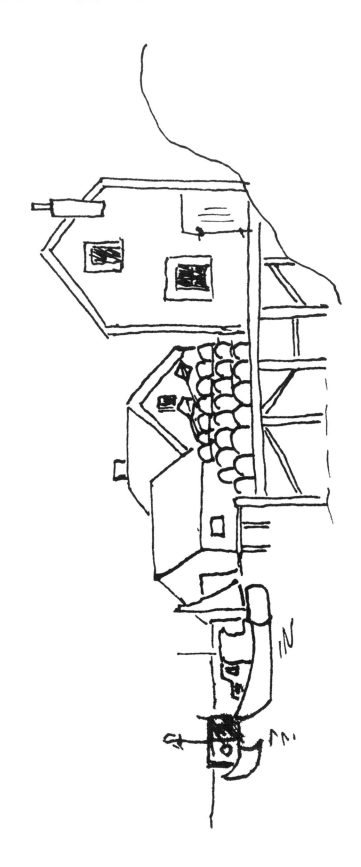

Awakening from Nightmares

Susie was expecting her friend Kevin to come to play when his parents came for a barbecue. She prepared a wading pool and tried out her swing and you could feel excitement bubbling out of her. Kevin arrived. He was taller than Susie, skinny where she was chubby, with a pained smile and a not-so-sure manner. He seemed very serious. They ran to the swing where Susie flew and Kevin fell and began to cry. When he noticed his mother looking, he began to wail. All better now — Mommy kiss! Mommy put you on the swing. But he couldn't get the hang of it while Susie was reaching for the sky.

She thought perhaps they should try something else and they both excitedly undressed to run through the wading pool. He wasn't too sure about that either, watched a few times, tentatively dipped his foot, went back for a run and with a tense strung body tried to copy Susie. She was fluid and joyful but he seemed to have no enjoyment or grace. Again he slipped and after a short time he began to shiver. Mommy found a towel, and it was time to eat.

Susie got the blanket spread for their "private" picnic and for a while things went smoothly as she mothered and tried to please, concerned that Kevin wasn't having a good time. But instead of his own hamburger, which had fallen on the ground a few times, he wanted a bite of his mother's. Dad wasn't paying much attention, immersed in a serious conversation with Susie's grandfather about American aggression in Iraq. Mommy then suggested a race around the house to "burn off some energy" and we all watched an overweight exhausted woman, a thin whining boy, and a little girl brimming with energy set off, disappear, and appear again. Susie pranced into view first.

"You know, he has all the toys you could imagine. He has so many he doesn't know which to play with. I have to hide some so he will forget and bring them out again as a surprise."

Kevin wanted another hamburger. His first was lying in the dust, the bun soggy with wading pool water. And he wanted to sit in Susie's grandfather's chair. He stood directly in front of the man, his mouth crammed full of bun, and said, "I want to sit there." He seemed perplexed when Susie's grandfather did not move. Later the man got up to find another drink but Kevin didn't notice then.

Susie, at last, seemed subdued, puzzled by the turn of events which had lost all fun and interest.

That night I had a nightmare: a huge pained face, tense and ugly, a mouth full of masticated mush, drooling and slavering but still screaming "I want. I want. I want." It was chasing me, devouring my world. I awoke suddenly and the rising sun was streaming through the bedroom window bathing it in early morning light. The trees were brilliant, the white birch shining out of their yellow green. I sat up and blinked, then lay back. Gradually the nightmare subsided and the image of Susie's joy and vitality returned and I got up.

Anna too was waiting for her friend. She sat with us, a face full of openness and childish wisdom. She looked right into you the way my daughter used to and still does sometimes. We talked of the humming birds that came to feed in the plastic flower above our heads, and of nuthatches — the upside-down birds. She was quiet, comfortable in the company of older people and we all had purple lips from blueberry popsicles. Jimmy arrived.

He was thin and tense but with a broad, toothless smile and blond tousled hair. I was struck again by the vast difference in vitality and awareness, by the grace of Anna and the awkwardness and hesitancy of the boy the same age. He fell, both off the bed when they were changing and while running through the sprinkler, and he cried though he tried to hold it in until he saw his mother. Anna, prancing and pirouetting in the spray, ran to help.

Again the blanket was spread, camping this time, mother Anna, at six, was already solicitous to sonny Jim but puzzled by him. Robin, Anna's mother, commented that girls ran circles around boys at that age, but a glance, tacitly agreed upon, suggested that she didn't think it changed much with age.

Not long after that I was driving the 401 east to the morning sun while listening to Stan Rogers.

California.
My friends all call you home.
If you take away another I'll be that much more alone.
Is it my fault that my kind are always drawn towards the sun
Like a child to home whenever darkness comes?

Joy comes in strange ways and I felt it surging over me for no reason, felt an almost physical and buoyant exaltation. I remembered Anna and Susie, Kevin and Jimmy. Is that what it is — the joy seemed missing in the boys? The real abandonment of self allowing the explosion of life to get out. Does it fade, can it be subdued so early?

It is said that our culture, born of a small, nomadic, paternalist tribe of Hebrews, denies death. My sense is rather that it denies life — denies the joy, the awe and the acceptance that radiated from Anna and Susie unaware of, but at the same time challenging, the fears that bound Kevin and Jimmy.

I'm going to get a new T-shirt and have a message printed on it: *Get Serious. Become Joyful.*

A year after meeting Kevin and my nightmare of him devouring my world I was jolted into remembering again, though not by him this time but by his mother. The circumstances were surprising and unexpected. I was involved in lambing. We had 500 ewes in the barn, about 50 to a pen. After the ewes had their lambs and cleaned them up (we had many sets of twins), they were removed together to single pens for 48 hours or so and then joined with the others who had lambed before. Lambing in a crowd was often confusing. Sometimes ewes about to lamb believe another lamb to be their own and a great mothering urge overtakes them. Restraining this behaviour is often required. One night the desperate look and frantic behaviour of a ewe, with the head of her own lamb out but determined to take over another's, bored right into me and brought Kevin's mother vividly and shockingly back to me. This behaviour has nothing whatever to do with the lamb but only the ewe's own needs. I was stunned by the image, by this frantic, fanatic, and unnatural need for mothering which *excludes* the offspring. It was a sort of waking nightmare as I struggled with the demented ewe oblivious to her own half-born lamb.

The story ends well, however. I got her out of the large pen and into a single one. By this time her lamb's head was grossly swollen but she settled down and I helped her finish lambing. The lamb could not even lift its head or suckle so we stomach-tubed him with his mother's colostrum. Three days later she and her now healthy normal lamb joined the others.

With 500 ewes lambing there are always lots of problems, lots of blood and afterbirth and shit, but mostly things go well. While the problems occupy you, the joyous gambolling and baaing of several hundred newborn lambs affirms the awesome miracle of life. As things taper off there is time to observe more quietly. One evening there was a small white lamb sitting contentedly in a large pen with no sign of its mother. Sometimes this too happens but the lamb was dry and quiet and seemed OK. But which of the 50 ewes was the mother and why in the hell wasn't she with her lamb? A ewe, with only the "toes" of another lamb out, appeared interested. It could be a twin coming. Hard to tell.

But as she rushed towards the lone dry lamb another ewe emerged from the group and gently cut her off staying between the now agitated stealer and the lone lamb. This dance continued for some time and I watched as things sorted themselves out. The single lamb was protected by her mother and the other ewe, with what seemed a sigh, went off to have her own.

I was intrigued by the mother of the lone lamb. She had had it quietly, cleaned it up, obviously fed it, and left it. But she guarded it firmly and gently. I left them alone. An hour later she came back to her lamb, clouted it with her foot to get it up to suckle, and then left it again. Once more that happened and that was it. The lamb was on its own. It knew its mother and she was there when he wanted her (it too turned out to be a ram lamb). No need to reinforce bonding or care for either the ewe or the lamb. They went directly into the pen with the other singles. In four hours I had witnessed the creation of an autonomous being. It wasn't Stan Rogers this time but an old and competent ewe which brought joy bubbling up as I watched her and realized what she was doing. Shepherds too sometimes need reminding of the joy, of the awe which life inspires. Another T-shirt — *Awe's right with the world*.

A Visit

Someone was approaching my camp along the far ridge on the other side of the lake. I couldn't believe it. I hadn't seen anyone for two weeks, since the pilot had dropped supplies — there was no one in this country. How could anyone get here? I was just above the tree line wandering about with my hammer tapping at rock outcrops collecting and mapping odd bits of magnetite and nickel ores — literally miles from anywhere. I watched for a long time as the figure moved along the skyline. He was moving fast it seemed to me and I waited in anticipation to see if he would come or pass by. When he got to the end of the lake he turned towards camp. Like Butch Cassidy, I thought, "Who is this guy?"

It was near dinner time when he got to me, a dark-faced Inuit with a rifle and a smile. *"Bonjour."* *Bonjour*? Who was this guy? He didn't have much French or English but seemed prepared to stay a bit. I indicated I was going to eat and would he join me. I had a forty-pound lake trout, partly eaten, stored in the last of the snow. It was hard to catch fish small enough to eat all at once.

We ate and sat a while and then he took a light skin from his pack, rolled over and went to sleep. The sun was high in the sky and I was still having trouble sleeping in the vague night of early summer at high latitude, so I sat a while longer by myself. He was the first Native I had met alone in his own country. I had known Indian guides and went to what I see now was a bogus boys' camp that pretended to have Indian roots. This man was something different. I was not uncomfortable in the bush but my little hammer was supported by a massive network of financiers, engineers, aircraft, pilots and supplies. He was alone with a rifle and I couldn't imagine where he had come from or where he was going. But I knew he belonged here and I felt like a stranger in the land for the first time.

Indian Givers, Native Roots, Stolen Continents, Occupied Canada; there are a lot of books being written now about Native people. At the time I had had the usual indoctrination at school; ignorant savages, we built and civilized this country, MacKenzie discovered the MacKenzie River — that sort of stuff. (Interestingly I met, later that summer, someone who was said to be Alexander's great-great grandson. And why not? It took one hundred years to acknowledge Admiral Perry's northern children and to admit he may not have reached the pole.) I was taught that this country has been "won in battle against vicious scalp hunters" which I now find, because of the ravages of disease, was rather like the British storming Belsen and conquering its occupants. "Heroic Beginnings" as described by Donald Creighton. But I had also had tuition from dogs and stars, song sparrows and sunsets and knew when someone was at peace in their world. This man was in another space, his competence and autonomy awesome in what I thought a hostile land.

Is that what it was that set off the rampage — their obvious confidence and sense of belonging in a wild and frightening land? Whatever it was, the truth of our behaviour is beginning to emerge and the psychic scar, the guilt, the denial, even in those who took no part but absorbed the propaganda, is buried deep.

A few years later I met an Inuit at a conference in Montreal who spoke some English. It was one of those typically manipulated scenes where invited Natives were asked "to explain themselves." I was uncomfortable and I could feel he was too. Later I met him wandering alone, desolate in the streets. He was muttering, "I cannot do it. I do not know how. They cannot hear. I am invisible." The words echo those of his ancestors and his children. He could not say to them, "Come north and share a meal with me alone in the tundra." We drank coffee until late in the night and neither of us went back to the conference the next day.

We came as strangers to a strange and terrifying continent, innocents, city people, outcasts. We were given gifts, taught to survive, welcomed. And we exploited, despoiled and plundered. Cartier kidnapped two Natives, Taignoagny and Agaya, took them to France and later returned with them to Montreal. When the crew began to die from scurvy, Agaya turned to a Huron woman for a cure and she virtually saved the whole crew from death. It happened where we were sitting. I did not know it then. De Soto used a Native woman, Lady of Cutifahiqui, as guide and then, after taking her gifts, enslaved her and robbed her people. And who can forget the image of Coronado mounted on his trusty steed, with 300 soldiers, 1500 other people, 1000 horses, 500 cattle, and 5000 sheep, led by a Native named Teh Turk — on a long chain? This, for me, is a picture that speaks a thousand words — this speaks of our true legacy. I am amazed now not only by the violence but by the almost pathological dishonesty we have inherited.

At one point I studied Jean Jacques Rousseau on my road to becoming a qualified teacher. To the Europeans who came here personal freedom did not have a long pedigree. Their most amazed descriptions of the New World was the freedom from rulers and from social classes based upon the ownership of property (stolen even then). For the first time they became aware of the possibility of living without the rule of a king! According to the Huron, the Europeans lost their freedom by their incessant use of thine and mine. "We are born free and united brothers, each as much a great lord as the other, while you are all slaves of one man. I am master of my body, I dispose of myself, I do what I wish, I am the first and last of my nation … subject only to the great spirit."

The contrast between the liberty of the Indians and the virtual enslavement of Europeans became the lifelong concern of Jean Jacques Rousseau and his *Discourse on the Origins of Inequality* in 1754. There was no mention of any of that in my rigorous training. "Of all the contributions America has given to the world, the idea of freedom from a social hierarchy has been the greatest. The idea that 'all men are created equal' is a gift to the world from the American Indian." (Robert Pirsig)

When Europe forged the ideas that became known as the Age of Enlightenment much of the light came from the torch of Indian liberty. The greatest radical to follow the example of Indians was Thomas Paine (1737-1809), the English Quaker. Egalitarian democracy and liberty are not Greco-Roman derivatives revived by the French in the eighteenth century. They entered modern western thought as American Indian notions translated into European language and culture. The Spaniards brought nothing of democracy with them, nor did the French and the Dutch who settled other parts of the world as well as North America. During the reign of George III, when the U.S. was fighting for independence, only one in twenty men (and no women) could vote in England. In all of Scotland only three thousand men could vote, and in Ireland no Catholics could vote or hold office. Amsterdam was ruled by 36 men, none of whom was elected.

Modern democracy is a legacy of the American Indians, particularly the Huron, Iroquois, and Algonquins; not British settlers, not French political theory, nor the failed efforts of the Greeks and Romans. Democracy was "here" when we got here, and nowhere else. Funny how we usually understand the phrase Indian Giver as someone who gives and then takes back. Do you call that a Freudian slip? Maybe what we mean is someone who is taken from and who is then made to disappear. It has been our way. I sometimes feel overwhelmed by anger at the depth of our dishonesty, at the deception, at being conned by slick salesmen. There is a land here crying out to be lived in but we have not yet found it.

We are strangers still and adolescents upon this earth. We are given gifts and guidance and respond with blind and brutal plunder. It is the same pathology. The planet guides all we do, we mimic its methods, copy its technologies, but we co-opt them to our own blinkered ends without understanding or acknowledging their depths. We cannot create so much as a blade of grass or manage the affairs of a single one of our cells. When democracy was brought forth, modelled upon the Iroquois Confederacy, the founding fathers forgot to include the council of grandmothers who chose the men to rule. The grandmothers, knowing small boys well, were the representatives of the seventh generation yet to be, and of the "Great Spirit" — the planet.

And we now, like adolescents, forget our own mother the earth which has brought us forth and gives us life. If that sounds too soppy for arrogant and fragile manliness, what in our own culture truly considers even our own children, let alone the seventh generation? And the planet? Well, the planet is for the taking.

I once took a course in logic at Harvard summer school. The professor stressed over and over again, "Examine your premise, examine your premise." Logic is the ultimate reductionist mode of thought which is often blamed for our troubled world. But if it is followed honestly, it too returns to the earth, returns to the mystery and the oneness. Newton and Descartes as scapegoats doesn't cut it. As Tom Berry is fond of saying, "The earth is primary, all else is derivative." The earth is the primary technologist, the primary inventor, the primary educator, the primary economist, the primary healer. It cannot be denied though deny it we do.

I did not know or think about these things long ago in the tundra. My friend (I call him that though I was with him only a day) was there in the morning and was brewing tea when I awoke. He indicated he was going north and east to the coast. He had no compass which was not much use anyway and could sometimes vary 20° in one hundred yards. I seldom used one either, the country gave you a feel for its direction. We left together and I walked a day with him. I could hardly keep up though he was not hurrying. Towards supper time we stopped and brewed up again, ate cold fish and bannock. Then he and his smile left as silently as they had come and I retraced our steps to my own camp.

His visit affected me for days — for years actually. My loneliness was different after he left and I tried to grasp the sense of his being. But I could not. It was not something separate or definable, it just was. Somehow he was like the arctic hares or ptarmigan and was just there, passing by, existing as they did. Though it sounds corny to our jaundiced ears he was at one with them, a part of the planet. There seemed no loneliness in him and I was puzzled. I was, I see now, envious.

As the summer passed I joined a small group in an assay camp and thought less about him in the bustle of daily busyness. But a chink had been opened to allow some light to shine upon the mystery I felt. Towards the end I began to get the message. What was wilderness to me was home to him. And he had seen and accepted me not as a stranger but as belonging. The difference I had first felt between us was in myself.

Often we sit on answers and can't get up to look at where we sit. Zen gurus and Tibetans roam this continent offering spiritual guidance. It is welcome and useful. But we sit upon the shoulders of men and women who were of the earth and lived as part of a sacred community.

There is a tendency, in our delusions of grandeur or fear, to scorn or romanticize Native Americans but there is a deep and powerful echo through all their lives. A culture with a trickster central to its mythology already has an advantage living on the planet over one with a vengeful god, or perhaps even one with a fat, benign teacher sitting under a tree. But more central by far is the foundation of the sacredness of life. To hold all life sacred is to acknowledge the unknown and accept the unknowable. When you are in awe of something you are not tempted to explain it away. And you are not then seduced by the half truths necessary to explain the unexplainable, half truths which now deceive us and infest all we do.

The Iroquois, the Cherokee, the Inuit didn't write about their world view, analyse it, struggle to contact it, agonize over alienation from it, build idols or monuments to it. There was no boundary between the sacred and the profane. They just lived, actively, in a sacred world. It was their being. Still is. When you come right down to it, what else is there?

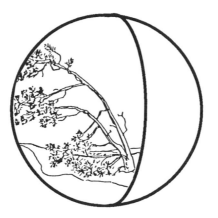

The Fluid Oneness of Things

S ometimes I just sit in the sun. I choose a tree on a southern bank and lean back to soak, my eyes open seeing the flash of a silver lake through green leaves, the clouds dissolving and forming, drifting in a blue sky. My mind stops and sometimes, some special precious times, I can hardly sense myself at all. André Brink's phrase "the fluid oneness of things" describes it best.

Albert Camus claims, "There is but one truly serious philosophical problem and that is suicide. Judging whether life is or is not worth living amounts to answering the fundamental question of philosophy." An extreme position, extremely self-absorbed perhaps but the essence of Camus' question, broadened beyond the prison of ego, remains the fundamental one. True values and ethics arise from the choice to affirm or deny life. They honour therefore not only all humanity but all of that which makes life possible. Indeed life itself provides the only context for value, for morality, for ethics. Denial of life, and more precisely destruction of conditions which promote life, presents the other choice.

The cult of the individual has defined personality in the western Christian tradition for hundreds of years. It sets people apart from one another and defines their interests in terms of the self in isolation — isolation not only from others but from the planet, and even, in a very real and curious twist, from themselves. For centuries it has been the individual which has dominated the meaning of personality and given guidance to ethics and morality — to the question of how we should behave. Theodore Roszac suggests, "There seems to be no way to be interested in the self that is not just an expression of self-interest. Individualism has laid a dark and stubborn curse upon all forms of self-discovery. It drives the person into a narrow fortress of the ego and locks it there; an isolated, opportunistic, ever watchful presence. No depth or mystery emerges, no inwardness beyond secret and ulterior motives. Filled with lavish self-importance but with little sense of self worth, measured by externals, by acquisition and conquest, by having but not by being, only the hard surface of self-interest thrusts forward against the legitimate moral need of the common weal."

The view of self as separate has led to the development of value and ethical systems which depend upon the theme of self-surrender or self-sacrifice because the self seems so truly at odds, so truly separate from the "common weal." It becomes a kind of battleground to balance self and non-self. To be unselfish in the service of some higher and external value — the pharaoh, the king, the country, parents — is to be virtuous, to behave morally. Selflessness, or denial of self, is equated with virtue and selfishness with evil.

It depends upon what we think is "good," as Nathaniel Brandon puts it. From the beginning, Brandon suggests, we are instructed that virtue consists not in honouring the needs and highest potentials of the self, but rather in satisfying the expectations of others by sacrificing them. "He's a good boy. He does what he's told." "She's a good girl. She behaves." The expression *God fearing* denotes goodness, with the ever present suspicion that the hard surface of self-interest has merely been softened a little to become enlightened self-interest. Morality consists mostly of "Thou shalt not," and is seen fundamentally as a *reactive* stance.

Camus asked his question imprisoned by ego, tormented by the horror Roszac so powerfully describes. He probably answered with a *no*, a reasonable response given the context and depth of alienation he embodied. If the self is seen as so evil, so alone, so empty, what other truly moral response is there but to destroy it? In the narrow anthropocentric and egocentric context of western religion, the Church, or at least something outside oneself, is considered the guardian of morals and serves in a very real sense, with guilt as the fulcrum, to restrain the ego. It was a losing battle from the beginning. Neither wisdom nor restraint is possible by "an isolated, opportunistic, ever watchful presence," when wants are endless and ethics merely a guide to behaviour.

The quest for a new moral basis, a new ethic, is still foundering on the same concepts of the individual as sovereign and separate and in need of some restraint for the common good. The solution is not there, though that is where the search is being conducted. It is doomed to failure. In his book *States of Emergency* André Brink writes, "To keep things apart, distinct, separate (man and woman; life and death; beginning and end), to define them in terms of their exclusivity rather than of what they have in common, must end in schizophrenia, in the collapse of the mind which tries to keep distinctions going." In this lies the failure of apartheid, and the failure, as I see it, of structuralism. What is suppressed, Carl Jung wrote, comes back to take a bloody revenge. And surely a most terrible revenge must come from the denial of the fluid oneness of things, in favour of the principle of isolation. Maslow describes it succinctly as, "Dichotomizing pathologizes."

In a world where everything is relative, everything connected and dynamic, there are no absolutes of the sort we are used to searching for. The search for a fixed reference is also doomed to failure. The place to search for solutions is simple. Look to the cosmos. Fifteen billion years of evolutionary example, of life supporting and life creating, can give the only absolute guidance and the only real reference. The earth story and its processes define our absolutes and ourselves and provide a moral basis for everyday life.

That is perhaps a simple place to start but then it gets difficult. We must accept what we imagine to be paradoxes. To be here at all requires differentiation, requires that we be separate. It is only in this way that the evolutionary imperative of developing potentialities can be served. Otherwise the result would be an amorphous blob or nothing at all! The universe has transformed itself from the simple to the more complex by differentiation. It is a fact, unalterable, and intrinsic. In diversity and complexity is the perfection of the universe.

Complexity requires levels and requires that they include and depend upon ones below. The complex is built upon *and includes* the less complex. The more complex is not and cannot be separate from the less complex. This is a fact. It is absolute. Thus diversity and unity are indivisible.

Codependency is its corollary — it is a fact. For example, photosynthesis depends upon two distinct cells, discrete structures which replicate by division, have their own distinctive DNA, synthesize their own proteins and are bounded by two-unit membranes. These kinds of cells are the fundamental units of all complex forms of animal and plant life. They are highly functional symbiotic arrangements, formed by absorption not digestion, totally dependent upon each other. Thus, existing forms of multicellular life have their origins in a symbiotic process that integrated a variety of micro-organisms into what can reasonably be called a colonial organism — the eukaryotic cells such as our own. We are processes invented over a billion years ago and they amount to the apparent paradox that unity and diversity are both required, are but aspects of the same thing! One cannot exist without being both separate and at one with the whole. If cells are "communities," what are we ourselves but larger "communities?" And are we not, beyond that, part of the community of Gaia? And beyond that? With all these levels of community, how can anything be separate? This dispenses with the fundamental conflict of self and non-self. We cannot be separate without being part of the whole and we cannot be part of the whole without being separate. No paradox there.

Mutualism, not predation, then, seems to be a guiding light of evolution. Conflict in nature between organisms has been popularly expressed in phrases like "struggle for existence," and "survival of the fittest." Few yet realize that mutual cooperation between different kinds of organisms — symbiosis — is more important, and that the "fittest" are those which most help another to survive. There is little argument that adaptation and competition exist but the idea that it is the foundation of life is a reflection of the limited view of Darwin and his times and indeed of the cult of the individual which preceded him and still dominates us.

Perhaps it is fear of life rather than the celebration of life which brings forth the cult of the individual and a survival of the fittest mentality. But neither pain, aggression, nor competition can explain the emergence and evolution of life. Life is by definition self-organizing and self-evolving, not only self-maintaining but self-forming. "Fitness" and indeed ethics, must be redefined by all life, and the sacred and absolute found in the processes of life. Lewis Thomas, author of *Lives of a Cell*, puts it this way. "A century ago there was a consensus that evolution was a record of open warfare amongst competing species, that the fittest were the strongest aggressors. Now it begins to look different. The greatest successes in evolution, the mutants who have made it, have done so by fitting in with, and sustaining, the rest of life. We should go warily into the future, looking for ways to be more useful, listening carefully for signals, watching our step and having an eye out for partners."

Contemporary biology leaves us with a picture of dynamic organic interdependence that proves to be far beyond what Darwin, or Huxley, ever imagined, perhaps beyond what can be imagined. Darwinism and its offspring, Social Darwinism, define life as competition and adaptation to the environment — as a reactive process. But the idea that life merely adapts is no longer tenable, neither is competition a successful means of survival nor a means of creating life. "Fitness" is not biologically meaningful in relation to separate, individual, or even species survival and adaptation. Left on that superficial level it becomes the horror of personal adaptive enterprise.

But it is just this posture which has been adopted by the western mind and the cult of the individual and gives rise to its decaying ethics and a planet in ruins. Life seen as merely reactive creates ethics that are merely reactive. The fact that Darwin was wrong, judged by present knowledge, obscures the revolution he did foster. He was perhaps less wrong than tempted to explaining what he could only describe. My impression is that he didn't even believe his own theory, as explanation, that is. But seekers create prophets, seekers for absolutes outside themselves imagined to be embodied in the prophet. Seekers demand explainers and the cult which ensues often obscures the teachings. It happened to Darwin and Adam Smith, even to Newton who, by his own admission, described gravity but couldn't explain it. And it happened 2,000 years ago to Jesus of Nazareth.

Mutualism is an intrinsic good by virtue of its role in evolution, and diversity is another intrinsic good. These are not human values but they provide humanity with a common basis and a link to common processes. Sacrificing diversity, indeed destroying it, as we do in areas ranging from corporations to satellite TV, in the name of unity or profit, is anti-life and misunderstands the need for both at the same time. Mutualism, self-organization and autonomy, freedom and responsibility, subjectivity, unity and diversity, spontaneity and hierarchical relationships based upon function and potential are ends in themselves. They do not need justification, they do not need moralizing, they do not need a code of ethics; they exist — and they define us and the universe.

The problem is, I think, that we do not truly believe life to be a dynamic and integral whole. We search for absolutes as if they were static and fixed — indeed as if they were absolute and as if they were separate. But it is only the processes which are absolute, and nothing is separate. There is a profound shift which arises with the change of context from static to dynamic, in which the process becomes the absolute. Death is inevitable, denial of it notwithstanding, and it is the part of life absolutely necessary for evolution. This takes some getting used to but it puts death in a different light because it is not death *per se* but destruction of conditions which promote life, which then becomes wrong, unethical, immoral and indeed anti-life. Earth processes then give us the only intrinsic and absolute basis for ethics, because they give us life. If process is sacred, its guidance can be brought to bear on everyday activity; it can guide the way we cut the forest or harvest fish. Done in a way which fosters life and the potential for life is ethical; done in a way which diminishes the potential for life, as we do now, is wrong, unethical, criminal. To cut a tree or take a life is not then wrong but to do it in a way which inhibits the emergence of new life is immoral. It is not so much "save the trees" as save the processes and conditions which create trees.

There is no conflict between being and becoming. Being is but a stage in becoming, an aspect of the dynamic process of life. How else can it be? How can things change and stay the same? It turns out they must change even to stay the same. Your friend whom you saw just last year has completely changed. Not one molecule of her face is the same as when you last saw her, all the protein in her body has changed. In six years she will have changed completely — yet she will still be your old friend, will she not? Perhaps it is these apparent paradoxes of life which cause confusion. Evolution demands death for life and life demands, indeed is, symbiosis and diversity demands unity. They are but aspects of the same thing. Rights are our own inalienably and responsibility is that which others should have more of. As individuals each organism has rights, but as inextricable parts of the whole each also has responsibilities and, try though we may, they cannot be separated. No paradoxes there. We have to have it both ways. It *is* both ways.

Ethics defined by an authority outside ourselves is impotent. And a cop-out. An ethics that affirms life comes from within and is focused outwards, not from without focused in. Paradoxes again but only apparent ones. And when you get right down to it, who needs ethics anyway? As separate selves we need them to balance the "common weal" but what if, in the manner of the planet, we transcend these two poles of self and non-self with a larger vision of ourselves.

Do you need a code of ethics to prevent you from cutting off your hand? When you truly comprehend that the rain forest is *your* lungs do you need a code of ethics to protect them?

Exhortations and moralizing are not only boring but unnecessary and are eliminated when the view of self expands beyond ego. The earth is primary, all else is derivative, to use Tom Berry's phrases again. It is there we find our guidance and our being. To know the earth story is to know ourselves and to honour ourselves and life. Ethics begins there, an active and not a reactive stance. Not how should we behave, how should we deal with the environment, how should we deal with other people, but what are we and what might we become? The choice, our choice, is Chardin's choice — "suicide or adoration."

Begin with the fluid oneness of things, with sitting in the sun.

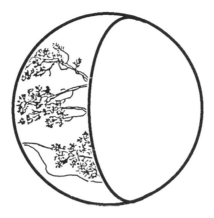

Balancing Act

L ife has been poised on the knife edge between chaos and order for as long as we can know about. Indeed, before life began the knife edge was evident. To slip off to either side, to chaos or to order, means the void, stagnation, a strange amorphous world of matter and antimatter — but somehow life is and planets and stars exist. Loren Eisley puts it best. "There is nothing in the world to explain the world ... nothing to explain the necessity of life, nothing to explain the hunger of elements to become life, nothing to explain why the solid realm of rock and soil and mineral should diversify itself into beauty, terror, and uncertainty." There is nothing to explain the rocks or minerals either.

Poor old Darwin got duped by the Church. He spent his life collecting stories, data, descriptions — the legitimate activity of science. But the Church was into the explaining business, for reasons of power and control that had little or nothing to do with the sacred. Darwin didn't understand Brock's Law, which existed even though I didn't, and imagined that science, to balance that power and control, needed to explain, could explain. The separation of Church and Science became one of conflicting explanations, the condition of opposites which Brock's Law describes as leading to stalemate. The Church had a franchise on an invisible cure for an imaginary illness and science, in the same vein, claimed to explain what can only be described. We have all, I'm afraid, been duped ever since.

Mathematics is one kind of language which can be used to describe things. But it is a curious game. What is *one* or *two* anyway? What is *one* telephone pole? If you look at a telephone pole as you walk along the road you know what *one* means. But get closer and then what is *one* ? Cells, lignin, molecules, atoms. Get closer still and it vanishes into the space between the neutrinos and mu mesons.

Go the other way and walk further down the road and the telephone pole gets smaller. Now draw back some more. A detailed map might show the house near the pole but draw further back and it vanishes again into the void. But in both cases the *one* telephone pole exists whatever that *one* telephone pole is. *One* is a descriptive convention — nothing more. It explains nothing. It is something we understand from our own perspective and on our own scale. *One* is both myth and metaphor.

Although it has always interested me, math has always seemed like a game: I have been able to do it, though I did not really understand it. I could manage the conventions and solve the practical problems which arose but somehow the problems seemed static and lifeless, limited and defined by what could be controlled and therefore solved.

Calculus as a language to describe changing situations somehow seemed curiously linear and fixed by initial conditions. Math, while appearing solid — *one* seems pretty concrete at first glance — seemed so also, in a way I could not determine and at the same time, flimsy. e.e. cummings, I believe, said that nothing that could be counted was important. You can see what he meant, thinking about love or fear but telephone poles! Curious that telephone poles too can only be counted from one place, one point of view and one scale.

Science and math are for power and control and the limits of both are denied or unrecognized. As Schumacher puts it so cogently, science becomes unscientific and illegitimate when it attempts to explain by theories that can be neither verified nor disproved by experiment. "Such theories are not science but 'faith,'" he says. We seem to have bumped into the Church again.

Not only is there nothing in the world to explain the world but there seems no math to describe anything but a selective and very limited predictable world either. Math, like science, is based upon a convention of objective order not balanced by either an acknowledgement of chaos or a way to describe it. If you like, we were stuck at half mathed — the math of order!

One day a man who spoke math as you speak your mother tongue was wandering beside a stream musing about whirlpools and eddies. They exist, as does a telephone pole, but seemed alive and chaotic while at the same time somehow ordered. Once we look for chaos we see it everywhere. He knew what whirlpools were just as we know what a cloud is, but how do you describe one mathematically? It seemed impossible, but from that moment in time, along with other people's separate autonomous musings, arose the mathematics of chaos dynamics and fractals — the geometry of chaos. We have a new language to describe dynamic change, a new language to balance the language of order, a new language to describe chaos and the order arising out of chaos.

Prigogine, in his book *Order out of Chaos*, likened classical science, and by implication math, to a disenchantment of the world. But now science, against its wish, has been "relieved of objective reality that implied that novelty and diversity had to be denied in the name of immutable universal laws. It is now open to the unexpected which no longer has to be defined as imperfect knowledge or insufficient control." Is the recognition of chaos a re-enchantment of the world?

I find it particularly exciting that this recognition has happened in our lifetime. But what floors me is the story it tells and the way it can serve new metaphors. Now I know math is exact and real and should not be used as metaphor. But numbers are metaphors — recall the one telephone pole and how exact and real that is. I think it permissible, in a world infinite in all directions, to use any metaphor to help expand the image of our life. What is exact? What is real, anyway?

The mathematics of chaos is based upon three ideas that are quite extraordinary, that seem to shout out its validity, its appropriateness to life. The first, the square root of minus one, would satisfy Loren Eisley. It is an imaginary number; it is unexplainable. There is nothing in the world to explain the root of minus one, nothing to explain what it is or how it can be used — but it can. It is a symbol which stands for the unknowable and is itself unknowable. How wonderful.

The second is the concept of an attractor. Nature, Max Planck claims, seemed to "favour" certain states, "does not permit processes whose final state is less attractive than its initial state." It appears, since the universe exists and has life, that this is a favoured state. Attractors give the mathematics of chaos a component describing an attraction to life.

The third is iteration: the use of a value determined from an equation that is put in again to find a new value, the new value then being put in again and again to build a picture — in short, feedback.

That process of iteration describes life. Begin anywhere, begin with atoms and the first iteration is molecules. Plug molecules in the equation of life and the next iteration is cells, and so on, each built upon and including the one before. Life is iteration based upon the unknown and we now have a mathematics with the same basis. We now have the beginnings of a mathematics of chaos to balance the old conventions of a mathematics of order. Together they can free our metaphors and make them more hospitable to dynamic evolution and change. Together they can describe the real world of order and chaos. Together they can describe the balancing act.

But there is still nothing in the world to explain the world.

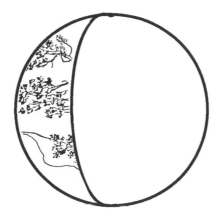

The Chairman and the Chokerman

They start you off as a chokerman. You scamper about in a jumble of logs, wait until the wire is near the one you want, then choke it, which means taking the spur wire and wrapping it around the log and putting the "ball in the socket" to attach it. You get out of the way, signal, and up she goes. Then you can stand a moment and stare off to the far hillside to wait for the next one. Where I was working there was not a tree left standing other than "sticks" which would do for trees in the east. These often got pulled down anyway by the big logs on their way to the top of the hill. It was massive destruction but we all pitched in anyway and, to tell you the truth, I enjoyed it. None of us saw what was happening. It was called "working in the weeds."

There was never, at any time, a sense of place, a sense of belonging. We were on the Charlotte Islands to do a job which had absolutely no relationship to place, or to the forest. None of us was going to live there — certainly not. Some worked hard, worked dry, and "pissed it away" in the streets of Vancouver until they had to sell their caulk boots and eventually stagger and shake their way back. Others worked quietly, sent money home and wanted only to get out to see the wife when they had a bit. I was there for the money. But I was also there as a volunteer for Frontier College and spent a lot of time teaching English to a group of Hungarians. I have been in the woods since I was a kid and had worked in many places in Canada as well as Sweden and Scotland but British Columbia was something else. High rigger, high technology country. The trees were so massive, the power of machines so great, we felt invincible. That was the sense of it — sheer power. Sheer arrogance.

Next, if you last, you can move up the hill and perhaps become chaser. Here you chase the choke at the other end to detach it and leave the log in a pile. If you're lucky, as I was, you can do two jobs and be chaser and second loader which means you also get to handle the huge tongs, to haul them a bit less than halfway along the log before it is hoisted onto a massive truck. In those days that meant $100 a day. And it was good work. On the move constantly, you needed to be very agile and keep your wits about you. It was dangerous. I loved it. But once, waiting in an unusual pause while the driver spoke to the "donk," a log slipped. It slid down the pile and struck another hard. The second log was fulcrumed by a third and it threw up another on its opposite end which hit me just below the belt, right on the right cheek. I was thrown ten feet in the air and landed, without my hard hat, in a heap on the road. Back to work, no problem, but it hit me later in the early morning hours how close I had come to death or permanent injury. Another time I had a "cherry picker" drop a log on me, I'm sure to this day, on purpose. He missed, but I had my hard hat on that time!

Some time after both these incidents, the safety officer lobbed a rock at me as I sat about fifty feet upwind of my work while the others smoked. Amazingly he hit me on the head and this time I didn't have my hard hat on, which was all he was ever concerned about. It was the only injury I had all summer.

Although I enjoyed the work, the men, the far mountains and the sea below, it got to me. No one else, other than the Hungarians, seemed to notice how detached it all was from the planet — if they noticed the planet at all. Noticed how utterly devoid it was of any conscious idea of what we were doing. It was segmented, separated, unthinking exploitation. We cleared the hillsides below the spar pole, the road sides with the "cherry picker," dumped the logs in the sea and shipped them out to somewhere. That was all there was to it. That was the name of the game and the planet would just have to survive as best it could, like me with my hard hat. It strikes me now the extraordinary state of limbo we worked in, as though floating in sleep, blinkered, our minds and eyes and ears oblivious, tuned only to the job at hand.

Recently, the chairman of one of the largest logging companies in Canada, and the world, said that they were "playing by the rules." And with an arrogant and sly smirk, he said, "If you change the rules we will change" — that is to say, we will carry on until you stop us! It gave me the shivers. I call that the Auschwitz attitude. I'm just doing my job; for killing Jews just substitute making profit for investors. And besides, those Jews are dirty, and they don't eat well, they even sleep all together in a heap, and those Indians are lazy, they burn the doors in their homes in winter to keep, warm etc. The attitude is pervasive and extends beyond people to the planet. Those trees are just standing money. I mean, look at them all over there on that far hill — there are lots of them. And they're next. But wait. As we scorn what doesn't fit, are we not burning our children's home to keep the fires of our own progress hot? Wendell Berry puts it powerfully: "Our present leaders — the people of wealth and power — do not know what it means to take a place seriously: to think it worthy, for its own sake, of love and study and careful work. They cannot take any place seriously because they must be ready at any moment, by the terms of their power and wealth in the modern world, to destroy it," except for their own private property, one could add. Applying Brock's Law allows a less personal, a less vituperative analysis: problems created by wealth and power cannot be solved by wealth and power.

One day I took a walk to the far hillside I had gazed at and looked back at our's. Amongst the giants, the clear streams, the small deer unmolested by predators on the Charlottes, I saw what we were doing. I had been over there labouring without a thought, making $100 a day, mindlessly tearing it apart. I didn't know any better — except I did.

I had cut trees in Sweden; indeed, I have felled more trees than the chairman I speak of. But in Sweden the land we worked was held privately as a pension fund for each generation. One cut was taken, selectively, and the forest stood for the sons and daughters, as it had for the parents. It was not our land but we worked it as though it was. We worked a land we felt we belonged to, inhabited by a spirit of oneness and continuity, although we too were just doing the job. We worked hard and productively but often paused with the horses — blankets, shirts, and breath steaming in the crystal cold — to just be where we were, to feel our life, our work and the forest as one. This was not articulated, any more than the emptiness and arrogance was in the Charlottes, but it was there. In Sweden we worked with the next generation in mind. In the Charlottes we worked as though there wasn't one.

There was a Norwegian about the camp. He was cruising the virgin forest, his assistant had gone squirrelly and he was looking for another. I got the job. It paid a lot less but took me to the damp rain forest amongst the nine-foot diameter spruce and the moss-covered ground. The salmon were returning and churned in the streams. I travelled the cathedrals of the Haida, running compass line with Thore following to estimate the stands. He knew the part of Sweden where I had worked and wanted to return to Scandinavia to cruise a forest he knew would stand. We both knew this one wouldn't.

We get stuck, don't we, in what we do, isolated and feeling impotent. We leave it to chairmen with their own agendas and imagine it has to be the way it is. His attitude will, in twenty years, be considered criminal, incomprehensible — perhaps even by his own grandchildren — and he a kind of a planetary Eichmann. But again one must look beyond the person — there will always be someone to blame. Focusing on a person leaves the nature of the corporation itself unquestioned. The chairman is a bought man and has been duped in a big way, forfeiting himself to an abstract belief in the corporation, a belief as strong and demanding as any fundamentalist religion.

And what of us? We all find it hard to get over to the other hill to look back at what we are doing. We cannot stop with the chairman, condemn him and not ourselves. We all now live separate from the earth which created and supports us, and we treat it with suicidal dishonesty. Safety is more than keeping your hard hat on, and living on the earth more than just adding a few environmental protection laws and blue boxes to business as usual. The same chairman claims to plant as many trees as are cut. Sounds good, but any tree planter knows the survival rates and the species planted and knows the half-truths that serve public relations. The pretence of job creation no longer holds and never did. A corporation is essentially a vehicle for making a profit for its investors. All else is contingency.

It is difficult to imagine how profoundly we must change. We are living dangerously and need our wits about us no less than a chaser and second loader. The chairman and the choker-man — we all now know, as I somehow found out then — we must walk to that other hillside. We alone can change the chairman's rules by changing our own — for his rules are indeed our own.

He was terrifyingly right — he is playing by the rules but the rules have nothing to do with the planet. He is fully prepared to exploit them for the selective short-term advantage of absentee shareholders. That is his honestly acknowledged job. But that's another matter — or is it? The Haida culture, where the wealth which was generated was kept or shared within its sphere, became destructive and perverted when that wealth was removed to serve other ends, other people.

We spoke of this, Thore and I, many years ago. I understood then the Haida frustration of being invisible and felt it myself. What are these people doing — can they not see? Will they ever belong anywhere? As we tramped the green, dark, damp forest our sadness grew. The Swedes who harvest in Canada do not harvest as they do at home. The Japanese preserve their own magnificent forest while exploiting others. Scotland was once covered with trees. Greece was too. Even Easter Island, that now barren speck on a broad ocean with the wind whistling unimpeded around the stone relics of a lost race, was once covered with trees.

Does the moon have trees? Is that where we will go next, where we will make a home, establish free trade, have Sunday shopping, indulge in trivial pursuits? Ask Neil Armstrong about the jewel he saw from space.

There amongst the silent spruce, the shadow of an idea emerged that those of us with callouses on our hands, and caulk boots on our feet, were not just doing a job. We were the bottom layer of an age-old attitude that denied our intrinsic, inextricable connection with all life. "This we know," said the legendary Chief Seattle. "The earth does not belong to man; man belongs to the earth. This we know. All things are connected like the blood which unites one family. All things are connected. Whatever befalls the earth befalls the sons of the earth. Man did not weave the web of life; he is but a strand of it. Whatever he does to the web he does to himself." This we imagine to be mere philosophy, unheard in our rush to turn trees into money, land into a commodity, and ourselves into consumers. Our pace and panic have hardened and intensified.

"We have become autistic," says Tom Berry. The dictionary defines autistic as "The tendency to daydreaming or introspection in which external reality is unduly modified by wishful thinking." Seems about right — a bit soft; we are hardly daydreaming — but right. But Tom means more than that. He means we are so locked up in ourselves that nothing can get in. "We are not talking to the river, we are not listening to the trees. We have broken off the great conversation. We are talking to ourselves."

"Working in the weeds," says a lot, doesn't it? But maybe we are beginning to come back to the earth, to return to the outports, to judge ourselves beyond jobs and possessions, to sense that we do, that we must, belong to the earth and are but a strand of the web. What we do to the earth we do to ourselves.

The timber cruising was drawing to a close. Thore and I broke out to the shore on our last day. We found a few leaning totems and a sea golden in the setting sun. We should have hurried back. It was late and we were far from the road but we brewed some tea and watched the sea otters and sat in silence for a while. Then we staggered out in the dark, as blind as a chairman or a chokerman to what we were doing.

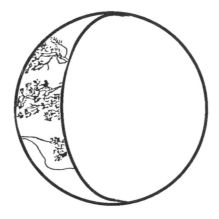

Dancing

Do men fear the autonomous? This question came to me as I was accompanying a friend, David, on his inspection rounds recently. He keeps 500 sheep who are guarded by two enormous dogs who stay with them always. They guard against coyotes, and our reaction to these critters and to wolves, which is strident beyond reason, gives us away. They kill, it is true, but so do we and much more wantonly. But I believe it is their cunning and independence that taunts us. They are autonomous and cannot be brought under our control.

I kept about thirty sheep once when I lived near Toronto. There were no coyotes but there were wolves nearby and I had a good ewe lamb taken by one of them. The sheep were in a field with a knoll in the middle and the lamb which "bought it" was away from the flock near the woods. I was working in the barn. The other sheep were not even disturbed and I didn't notice until evening. It was magnificently done. But the local reaction was one of outrage not admiration. Wolves — kill them all. Dogs on the other hand can be viciously indiscriminate killers. They worry sheep to death, chase the whole flock and appear to kill just for the sake of it. But dogs somehow escape with an "oh dear," as though it was a matter of simple truancy. But then dogs generally do our bidding.

There is a curious reaction to David's guard dogs amongst local sheep producers which amounts to a virtual denial that they do the job of protecting the sheep. It is almost as if the dogs were depriving them, in these times of anger and unrest, of an enemy they can focus on, to hate or to blame. They don't want to know about the dogs and prefer to solve the coyote attacks with government funded $10,000 night scopes, or intrusive machines with electronic noises and flashing lights. They are losing quite a few of lambs and mostly they just want the coyotes dead. My friend with the guard dogs on the other hand has lost only one lamb since the dogs came, and a disgruntled neighbour is suspected of that one, though he lost many before.

I was looking forward to seeing the dogs. My experience with sheep and aggressive working dogs led me to expect to see the dogs keeping watch over the sheep — outside the flock, in control as it were. As we approached the field I could see the sheep but the dogs were not in evidence. David pointed them out to me. Both dogs are white and they were lying right within the flock. It was extraordinary. The only difference seemed to be that they were not chewing their cuds! It is one of my favourite sights, a quiet flock on a grassy knoll, and there amongst them was the enemy.

These days we use the word *independent* enthusiastically and talk of fostering it but our actions belie our words. We believe, ultimately, in power and control — and have done so for a very long time. And we have made the world unsafe for autonomous life and for a subsistence way of life which denies our control. I expected to see it myself, to see the dogs in control . There seems no better image or metaphor for another way than two huge dogs lying amongst sheep.

Ivan Illich talks of a "500 year war against subsistence," but it goes much further back than that. In England, from the time of the Norman Conquest, knights and overlords began to gain control over the land called the "commons." Legislation helped make it legal . Later, aided by wool merchants who found more profit in sheep than in autonomous people, it crippled the sustainable agriculture of many districts which was rationalized in the name of efficiency and higher production. Karl Polanyi points out that the enclosure of the commons in the eighteenth century created the rural homeless and, thereby, the first industrial working class. It was disaster for both human and ecological systems and a blow against autonomy. People became dependent, under control, and land became a commodity, not the foundation of existence.

Garrett Hardin, who talks of the tragedy of the commons, fails to note that the commons was a social institution and was never without rules. The effects of overuse were clear to those who depended upon it. Hardin's famous "Tragedy of the Commons" turns out to be only the tragedy of consumerism, which he takes for granted. His misunderstanding and the unawareness by most of us of what we have lost is the real tragedy. The commons was the basis for an autonomous existence but it required the acknowledgement of the mutual dependence of people and planet, something we seem to find impossible to imagine. The word itself deceives and separates us from the earth. It was, as Gary Snyder puts it, "a curious and elegant social institution within which human beings once lived free political lives while weaving through natural systems — a level of human society which includes the nonhuman."

It was a disaster for native people here when the privatizing mentality arrived in North America with the Europeans. They found an autonomous subsistence culture, sustainable and harmonious, with a vast system of common land. They found more democracy than the common man had at home, where women had none. Here there was more respect and equality amongst men and women. They found a healthier, a happier people. A more subtle people. They found an autonomous people. The enclosure of the commons in England, when one acre in seven was *taken* into private ownership, pales in comparison to our treatment of the native commons. The vicious and wanton behaviour of Europeans in the Americas cannot possibly be explained in rational terms and reveals a deep fear of the autonomous.

It reached near hysterical proportions and continues to this day as local people in other undeveloped places are literally blasted from their homes by international logging companies and national governments. Those trees, those people are "not doing anything productive," just living. Can we really pretend that what we do is being done to improve their lives? Legislation and force continue to support efficiency and higher productivity. Thousands of Philippino dead from a recent mud slide attest to a direct and brutal result. The recent death of tens of millions of monarch butterflies is a more subtle effect, of 'efficient' land use. The attitude extends to and now encompasses the whole planet and all we do. Even science, begun as a search for meaning and wisdom, has become merely science for control. We have woven an intricate web for our own deceit.

A Haida elder is said to have asked, "When are they going to behave as if they were going to stay here?" It is a crucial question. For *to stay* here means to sustain, not to exploit and control. Pick any resource issue, indeed almost any issue at all, and you will find behind the rhetoric, "words are but wind," as my granny used to say. Behind the rationalizations is a fear of the autonomous. Ted Turner, creator of CNN, said in a recent and incredibly honest interview, "I have never known a successful man who was not driven by insecurity." Is it this insecurity which fears and tries to drive out the autonomous?

Snyder calls for a recovery of the commons. "Understanding the commons and its role within the larger regional culture is a step towards integrating ecology with economy." But that would require that the fear of autonomy be exorcised. This is strongly resisted in the name of free trade or a global economy or whatever. Take over the world rather than allow autonomy and lose control! The results will be as disastrous to both social and ecological systems as were the enclosures. But Snyder is more eloquent in his plea than the merely rational idea of integrating economy and ecology. "Take back that which defines our larger being, regain the personal, local, and community 'commons', take back direct involvement in sharing the web of the wild world — or that world will silently slip away." There is no mistaking his vision.

Do not imagine that this fear of the autonomous is focused only on enemies, on primitive or common people, or that it always exists somewhere else. We have taken childhood from our own children. This time of curiosity and untroubled joy has been regimented, controlled and enclosed by the fences of our own fear, too. Schools, which we see as benefiting children, more often imprison them and make them dependent. We focus on data and right answers conspiring against independent intuition and creativity though all the while proclaiming their virtues. Perhaps "kids' crime" is a struggle for relief from a far greater crime.

It is a long, sad trail and goes back, perhaps, to the first warring outcasts envious of the stable, often maternal but mostly partnership societies of very ancient times. Is it the fear of being an outcast perhaps, coupled with what Tom Berry calls a "deep resentment" of the conditions of life? In any case, the barbarians are no longer at the gate, they are now ourselves or act on our behalf.

The dictionary defines autonomy as self-governing or independent, which in today's world is, at the very least, naive. In biology autonomy is defined as "not influenced by another organism." This is impossible and gives us away. No organism can exist without being dependent upon other life — and higher organisms are communities of other life. From the very beginning of life, autonomy has been coupled with mutual support. Even DNA, supposedly *self* replicating, cannot do it without protein — and cannot create that protein. Brock's Law strikes again. It is not one pole of autonomy balanced by another of support, not a few supported by many, but both together, both autonomy and mutual support, neither possible without the other. For is not autonomy, diversity and mutual support, unity? This is not idealistic. It has nothing to do with ideals but is a fact and condition of life. Our fear is a fear of ghosts we dream ourselves.

Our sheep rounds became a ritual dance. Since the dogs stay with the sheep, feeding time is in the field. Two enormous white animals, Buddy and Shep, emerged from the flock bounding towards us. A chunk of meat and a pile of kibble was put out for each of them while we stood in between. A few sheep, usually the same ones, began to circle closer in the knowledge that some kibble is always missed. Sometimes the dogs changed piles just to check out what the other was getting, their own growling and skirmishing by now ritualised. Feed was portioned out slowly. We talked and looked at the sheep. One hunchbacked ewe, missed in several culls, was noticed so often she seemed to be ten. The dogs looked at us too from their breakfast tables and wagged their tails. With breakfast over the dance began in earnest, prancing and squirming, if big dogs can squirm. They leaned against us, almost pushing us over. The circling sheep, pretending not to look, moved closer. It was a fine time.

At the end, Buddy puts his paws on David's shoulder, his huge head level but bigger by far, and a real dance begins. I could just hear David singing "Put your head on my shoulder." Both are autonomous, there's very little question of that. Can you imagine *making* a dog like Buddy stay with the sheep to guard them? And both are dependent one upon the other, of that David has no doubt. The coyotes keep trying and they too survive. It is a dance that has been going on for fifteen billion years — the dance of life.

Joe Said

J oseph Campbell called to us in our wilderness of doubt and said to follow our "bliss." What could that possibly mean? It turns out he was his best example and arrived through many trials at wisdom known in childhood. It was, they say, a hero's journey.

Do poems need always have the same number of lines per stanza, or rhyme perfectly? Maybe not. Perhaps each of us is meant to follow a different path.

At thirteen Joseph Campbell was fortunate to become sick and could not go to school. He was left to his own devices and to a timeless time of morphine and dreams — and to the care of a wise old man who knew the ways of nature and was an Indian at heart. His later journey, on the surface an intellectual one in halls and lecture rooms, appears conventional. Conservative almost. But revolution was peeking out for those who heard his soul.

And after eighty years he was a a TV star, a grand old sage, a guru for a nation. "Tell me. Is it meaning we all seek?" the talk show host enquired as if referring to the weather. He believed Joe's reputation to be focused on intellect and meaning. It is our myth. It seemed his life. "Well no, " Joe said. "It is *experience* we seek. Deepening and opening the experience of life."

Meaning, the preserve of experts, priests, and professors is not it! Joe, what have you said?

Experience is available to us all and any deep experience brings within it the divine. We each can seek the sacred in ourselves and find it on our own by being open to all life.

Joe said.

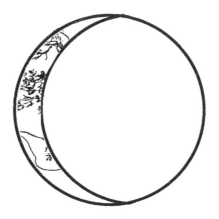

Letter to My Daughter

Dear Laura,

I have dedicated this book to Tom Berry on one side and you on the other with me sandwiched between mentor and daughter. That is as it should be. We share an allegiance to the planet and to the dynamic of the evolutionary adventure.

Our whole culture conspires against a search for a deep sense of being. It is damned difficult to even begin the search which is ultimately lonely and frightening, especially with the poverty of opportunity available. Or apparent poverty. If you learn only from the culture, from school, from TV, from business, forget it — you will be forever frustrated and superficial. Welcome to the West! But if you can allow the planet to speak to you and through you, you will not necessarily find it less difficult, but there will develop within you a sense of comfort — it's the best way I can describe it — a sense that you belong. Though the effort is often painful it brings forth joy. "Suppose," as Roszac puts it, "the whole of creation began to speak to you in the silent language of a deeply submerged kinship ... " It is what we can aspire to.

We are bombarded by data, by propaganda. The solution to garbage loads of data — the Information Age leads to paralysis — is selection based upon a deep experience of your own sense of yourself. You are informed by experience not "factoids," to use Bill McKibben's term.

Trust it. Without that sense, begun and continued always by your own searching, you cannot be other than overwhelmed and remain always detached, always a spectator. A career, a BMW, a monster home, to do well for yourself seems such a little life. For some reason I might have suspected such poverty early in my life because of a passion for life. Those lowly expectations, a kind of voyeurism as you have sometimes suggested, have impeded our deeper integration with the planet to the point, now, where the future of the planet, and the voyeurs, is threatened. There is no survival strategy but to go deeper, to participate as a member of the planetary community, to have the courage to embark on your own journey to the unknown. It is a matter of story as Tom says but also a matter of courage. I like Ray Bradbury's line, "Is there no rest? No, only journeying to be yourself."

The planet is the great teacher and we are at last being forced to hear. You are fighting your way through the garbage. Welcome. We need you. You are miles ahead of me at your age and that too is as it should be.

In my youth there was absolutely nothing to show the way. In fact there was less than nothing; there was what Pirsig calls a "cultural immune system" which rejected foreign notions. Everything was kept firmly on the surface or kept hidden.

Religion conspired to bury the sacred, education conspired to submerge learning, business conspired to turn us all into consumers and isolated, but not autonomous, cogs in a production machine, and fathers conspired to reproduce their likeness. My generation in this culture, tutored by the ones before it, has developed the narrowest, most uninspired, most tight-assed vision of ourselves in the history of human consciousness. We do not look in, we do not look out, we gaze only into the mirror of our own self-interest. Tragic though this is, the view from the other side of the mirror of all this posturing and preening is not exactly giggle free.

For some reason I could never buy any of it. Who was that ten-year-old who rejected it all? Where did he come from? I have no idea — but life spoke to me quietly amidst the shouting. I have tried to explore here some of what I do know of the roots of my own immune system which rejected the culture and heard music with a cosmic beat instead. And I have tried to understand the guidance the planet offers.

Perhaps what we do in life is try to recapture the wisdom of our earliest years, before mind and culture, when experience was what we knew. Who was the three-year-old who was you who could look into others' souls and not turn away?

This book is perhaps not up to beer and talk or a quiet ski together on a lonely lake but it covers more ground and you can keep it by your bedside! As always I encourage you to be what you can be.

With love,
Peter

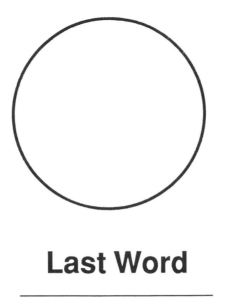

Last Word

Many authors are mentioned in these variations and a few books. Hundreds of books are not mentioned. In academe it is *de rigueur* to list all references to support an argument, to support your position as expert. I am not an academic or an expert and *Variations on a Planet* is not an argument — it is a story. It is not put forward to convince you, which I couldn't do anyway, but so that you might recognize some of my stumbling in your own.

I myself continue to stumble, and to read, and to recognize ideas and I get great comfort from them, curiously even the unpleasant ones. It is perhaps more common than is admitted but I seldom read for instruction and I seldom use bibliographies to pursue a topic. It seems I read to encounter ideas I have had or are somehow there to be recognized and I never know where I will find them. Somehow, I come across books that are appropriate or authors who strike a chord and I read everything of theirs I can find. Over the years this has given me great pleasure and I write partly to return the favour. Writing, too, reveals ideas I sometimes didn't know I had, and sometimes words come and cannot be written down fast enough and disappear. Equally, I can read right through a passage and not comprehend it. A different day, a different life, a different story. This wonderful, moving, transforming, unfathomable life cannot be encompassed by anything but story. Ain't it grand?

So ... if you found a phrase that clicked with an author's name near it, go to the library and check out what's been published. And write yourself — you never know what might come out.

And

Listen to Albinoni.

Look at a rain drop on a hemlock branch.

Paddle against the wind.

Sail with the wind.

Check out the Mayflowers at the edge of the snow.

Ride a bike in the country.

Build a cabin.

Climb a tree.

Welcome the song sparrows back.

Cook a meal for your mother.

Send her a birthday card on your birthday.

Imagine you're a gannet.

Go into the woods in May and curse the blackflies.

Smile at somebody who doesn't expect it.

Learn to play the guitar.

Ponder the fact that water is heaviest at 4°C.

Imagine if it wasn't.

Run in the rain.

Skate around a five-mile-long lake.

Make beer.

Tell a story.

Tell your story

to yourself.